Give Me That Old-Time Religion

Give Me That Old-Time Religion

MARTHA CHILDERS HUMBARD
with Bill Armstrong

LOGOS INTERNATIONAL
Plainfield, New Jersey

GIVE ME THAT OLD-TIME RELIGION
Copyright © 1977 by Logos International
All rights reserved
Printed in the United States of America
ISBN: 0-88270-227-0
Library of Congress Catalog Card Number: 77-80161
Published by Logos International
Plainfield, N.J. 07061

Give Me That Old-Time Religion

1

"Rex, we sure gave the devil a black eye, didn't we?" I chuckled, standing next to my son on the platform. "It's about time Old Slewfoot got what was coming to him!"

Rex had just burned the last note on a 12.5 million dollar mortgage at the Cathedral of Tomorrow. To add to this victory celebration, the service was being telecast to millions of viewers all across America.

Everywhere I looked people were laughing and crying and raising their hands in thanksgiving to the one who had delivered the Humbard ministry from the oppressor. As the one hundred-voice choir sang "To God Be the Glory," four thousand faithful believers in the congregation stood to their feet and joined in a mighty chorus of praise and worship. The huge lighted cross that hangs from the domed ceiling of the Cathedral never looked more beautiful.

Rex and Maude Aimee gleamed as they hugged each other, tears streaming down their faces. They weren't the only ones. All the Humbards, from granny down to the youngest great-grandson were rejoicing and carrying on. And we had a right to.

This marked the end of a two-and-a-half-year battle that had kept my son's ministry under tight government restrictions and had threatened to close it down for good. After twenty years of financing the television program by selling bonds, Rex had been notified one day by the government that he was in violation of certain security laws because the Cathedral's security notes were not registered.

When this happened Rex was not delinquent on any bills, but suddenly he had to have enough money to cover all the notes should they be cashed in one day. It's almost like the bank coming to you on your house and saying you had to have enough cash to pay off your mortgage in full!

It was a real blow. You can imagine the shock of being suddenly faced with a 12.5 million dollar debt to the government. Across the country the media picked up the story, and we were given bad publicity just when we needed people to stand behind us.

As rough as it was, it wasn't anything new to us. We knew it wasn't any battle with the government or the media or the banks. It was a definite move by the devil to rip into shreds and destroy this ministry that God himself had ordained. It was a battle as old as time itself.

One thing's for sure though, the victory we were celebrating had not come without a price. It had cost untold hours and days of prayer and fasting, not only by Rex, but by everyone connected with his ministry.

I remember one afternoon during that period when I walked into Rex's office. It must have been one of the darkest hours of his life. He was sitting there all alone, with his face in his hands and a look of such deep despair. I said to him, "Son, just remember that Romans 8:28 is still in the Bible."

"I know, Mom," he answered. "But I sure don't see how any good is going to come out of this."

But good did come out of it. Millions of TV viewers and our many friends in the various churches and ministries across the country had rallied together as one big family and helped defeat the devil. God is always faithful to hear the prayers of His children, and once again we knew it to be true. Once again He had extended His hand to us and the devil had been turned aside. In all these years of serving the Lord and coming against all kinds of opposition, victory had never tasted sweeter than on this day.

Through tears of joy, I walked back to my seat on the platform. As I continued to praise the Lord, the Holy Spirit began to bring to my remembrance the many times Satan had tried to discourage and defeat us, and how each time the Lord had delivered us.

I thought about the time in Carrollton, Illinois when I was warned that if I got up to preach again, my head would be blown off with a shotgun blast. I did what I had always done under pressure. I went to my Father on my knees. He gave me His assurance of protection, and I preached that night while the other members of our gospel team were down under the platform on their knees undergirding me in prayer.

I thought about the beautiful red dress with the black velvet trim I liked so much. A friend had given it to me, and it was the first time I had worn it. I had gone into the tent before the service and was praying at the altar rail, when all at once I felt something hitting me on the back. Someone had slipped into the tent and thrown rotten eggs all over me in an effort to discourage me from preaching that night. That hadn't stopped me either.

I remember the time my son Clement had been beaten because he dared to preach the truth of the gospel, that Jesus is coming back soon. And the time that Dad Humbard had been whipped by a mob of hoodlums and left for dead along a railroad track. He would have bled to death, but again God sent an angel to rescue him. Once dynamite was placed under the building where Dad Humbard was preaching. The charge failed to go off because God had sent His angel to prevent it. Over and over again the attempts of Satan have been turned aside. God has been so good!

I still remember the cold tents and dirt floors and the endless miles on the road between towns in cars, trucks and trailers. At one time, there were more than twenty of us Humbards traveling together from one end of the country to the other. We lived from day to day, not knowing if there was going to be enough money left over after the bills to buy food and gas.

I can see how God planned all those years from the beginning to prepare us for what we now see coming into reality.

As I listened to Rex's words, and thought about the people at home in front of their televisions, I knew that the goal that had always been before me was being fulfilled in a wonderful way. Here we were in Akron, Ohio, and yet millions were being reached by these telecasts every Sunday morning.

When I began to preach, I had no idea that the day would come when we could stand before TV cameras and reach so many people at one time.

I have seen many of the things that I preached about years

ago come to pass, and even though I didn't foresee TV, I'm not surprised at it , because it's the perfect way to reach the world with the Word of God. I've always known that all things are possible with God and it has been this sure knowledge that has kept the years of serving God exciting.

As I listened intently to Rex's preaching, I remembered the times when he would grow tired of being around so many people and wish he could move out on a farm some place where he would never have to see people again. That feeling would only last for a short time because he always had such a burden for lost souls he could never isolate himself from the world. He *had* to tell what God had given him, and he had to reach souls for Christ. It is there inside him, as it is inside our whole family because God put it there.

Often, as I listen to Rex or Clement preaching, they sound so much like their dad that it just wrings my heart. I can see how God has surely multiplied what Alpha and I had begun. Over and over again the devil has tried to subtract what God multiplied, and at times it would have been easier to just quit and go back to the hills of Arkansas to raise chickens and hogs. But then, that wasn't what we were called to do.

As I sat there on the platform with my memories, I was swept back in time. I could see how God had prepared my children to serve Him. Then I looked back further and saw how He had begun preparing me.

I was just a small baby when my mother died. But before she went home, she prayed that God's protection would always be around me, and that He would lead me all through my days.

I could clearly see myself as a lonely child growing up, fighting for a place in a large family without a mother to fight for me. I was just a bit of a girl; brown-haired, freckle-faced, and always fighting for something. And then He gave me what I longed for more than breath itself. He gave me His love and filled me with His sweet Holy Spirit. From that moment on, I was totally committed to Him.

That commitment has brought me into many dangers, and a life without the material blessings that most women look for, but there has never been one minute of regret. The years have raced by; the goal has always been before me, and I have never tired of reaching for it. The goal, of course, has been to reach the lost with the Good News of Jesus' redeeming love.

I know that the kind of life we lived was not always easy for our children. One year, Juanita, our youngest child, was in seven different schools. The children didn't complain, and they were able to take it all in stride. Without those experiences the ministries they now have would not be possible.

Working for the Lord is a way of life, but not the easy or glamorous way. There is a lot of hard work, late hours, lack of privacy, physical and mental fatigue, a lot of giving and a lot of persecution. But it's all so worthwhile!

All of the dirt, grime, sweat, and sawdust comes back as a sweet fragrance in my memory, for the years have a way of smoothing out the rough edges and taking away the bitterness.

We have had a lot of battles over the years but many more victories. Yes, over the years we've given the devil a lot of black eyes, in spite of all of his efforts against us. His business is to try to stop us while our business is to win, and to never stop believing that all things are possible with God.

A few years ago I was being interviewed for a magazine

article, and I was asked what I believed and preached. At that time I told the reporter, and I don't mind repeating it again. I believe in the Bible from the first word of Genesis to the last word in the Book of Revelation. I believe in the old-time religion which I still preach. I believe that you are saved from the top of your head to the soles of your feet. You're honest, you walk uprightly and you don't want to beat anybody. They could put you in a bank with all the doors open and all the money within reach and you wouldn't take a penny. That's the kind of religion I believe in. Give me the old-time religion.

The old-time gospel is all our family has ever known. This is what we preach and this is what we live by.

Rex was now wiping his eyes and stepped to the mike again. "People might say a lot of things about Rex Humbard and the Cathedral of Tomorrow, but no one has ever said we are not soul winners. This is the heartbeat of our ministry.

"This morning I am happy to announce that beginning in two weeks, every Sunday, my message will be translated into Russian, Chinese, Japanese, French, Spanish and Portuguese. Every sermon I preach from this platform will be broadcast by shortwave radio and television on every continent on the face of the earth!"

Again my eyes filled with tears. God had not only given us a tremendous victory this day, but He had been using these past two and a half years as a preparation for reaching the whole world with the gospel.

The devil had been given more than a black eye. He had been dealt a knockout blow!

2

From the time I was born around the turn of the century to Anna and John Childers on a farm near Chillicothe in northern Missouri, God has had His hand on my life.

People often ask me my age but I really can't tell them. When I was about eight months old, my mother died and time slipped by so that no one could remember exactly when I was born. My brothers and sisters would get into big arguments about my birthday, but I didn't even have a registered birth certificate. I've written to every office that I can think of and no one has a record of my ever being born. But I have this confidence. God has my name written down in the Lamb's Book of Life and that's all that really matters.

I was around seven or eight years old when my brothers and sisters decided I needed a birthday, and so they picked May tenth. How exciting to finally get a birthday! I went around telling everyone I met, "I have a birthday!"

We had a good friend whom all of us kids called Aunt Lizzie. One day we went to visit her, and all at once I remembered I hadn't told Aunt Lizzie that I had a birthday. She was standing in front of her big cast-iron stove cooking supper.

"Guess what, Aunt Lizzie? I've got a birthday," I announced.

"Well, Martha, everyone has a birthday," she replied.

"I know, but before I didn't have one, but now I do!"

Then she began to show some interest. "Well, just who gave you one and when is it?"

"It's May tenth," I answered proudly.

"Now Martha, I know for a fact your birthday isn't May tenth."

My heart dropped. Aunt Lizzie was taking my birthday away from me. I puckered up and started to cry.

"No, Martha, your birthday couldn't have been May tenth. I know because I was present when you were born. It was in February and there was a big snow on the ground. I don't remember the exact day or year, but it had to be somewhere around the middle of February. I'd say the fifteenth or sixteenth. So Martha, why don't you just take February sixteenth for your birthday."

That made me happy again, and I ran off to tell others. February sixteenth has been my birthday ever since, even though I still can't tell you that is the exact date or how old I am.

A short time after this birthday incident, a friend persuaded my father to trade his large farm near Chillicothe for a farm he had never seen in Arkansas.

I can still remember that trip. The whole family set out for Arkansas in two covered wagons and a buggy, a good 450 miles over twisting, turning dirt roads.

20

When we reached the southern part of Missouri, we had to cross the swift Eleven Point River. My father said to my brother, "Willy, that current is strong and the buggy is light. It could pull the horse down. You get in the back of the wagon and lead the horse from there where it's safer."

Sure enough, as we were crossing the river, the horse fell and nearly drowned. My father tied a log chain around his waist and waded out in the water with a knife to cut the harness from the horse. Despite the horse's pawing with his front hooves, my father was able to hold his head up. Somehow he managed to lead the horse out, and then tied the chain to the buggy and pulled it out.

In a few days, our little caravan rolled into Arkansas. But we stayed only a few years because father wasn't pleased with the new farm at all. He said, "I wouldn't live where I don't have a neighbor." The nearest neighbor was two miles away and he was deaf and dumb. So we moved to Egypt, Arkansas for a while until father could arrange to move back to West Plains, Missouri.

Those early days in West Plains before I found the Lord were often painful. Many nights I'd go out behind the barn, the chicken house, or in the orchard and cry my little heart out. My heart felt so empty without a mother. I'd see children who had mothers and thought how wonderful it must be. And I figured they didn't even appreciate what they had. How I longed for a mother's love!

One evening, a lady stopped by the house and asked us if we would like to go to a church meeting. It was what they used to call a "union meeting." Most of the West Plains ministers would get together and have an evangelist come in and hold a week of meetings. I was glad she invited us, and hoped I'd find something special that would fill my emptiness.

There was a big a tent and what looked to be half the town seated under it on benches. The children were led up to the front seats and after a while a man with a pleasant smile approached us with a pad and pencil. "What church did you come to join?" he asked.

Well, I didn't know any more about joining a church than a hog knows about a side saddle so I didn't say anything. Finally, after a long moment of hesitation, my sister Hattie spoke up and said, "I guess the Christian Church. We'll join the Christian Church."

But that didn't seem to do us any good. They baptized us and that was it. There didn't seem to be anything spiritual about it. It was a big church with over 1,250 members, but they never prayed for us, or told us about God's plan of salvation. The members all went to shows, smoked pipes and cigarettes, drank and did just about everything the world did. They just joined the church and said they were going to live better, but there was no difference in their lives.

I didn't last but two weeks there. I guess my mother's prayers were so strong on me that God wanted me to get in the right channel instead of getting satisfied with a salvationless religion.

A year later, my brother Charlie was taking Hattie and me to the carnival that had come to town. Right across the street, on the very site of the union meeting the year before, there was another tent meeting going on.

That was really where I wanted to go, but Charlie insisted we had to go to the carnival. But since we had come a little early, we slipped into the back seats, and sat in on the

22

meeting a little while.

"This is what I want to do. I don't want to go to that old carnival," I told Charlie. This meeting was so different from the union meeting. The people were singing and the glory of God was all over their faces. People of all ages were testifying of the love of Jesus and telling how they had found the Lord and how their lives had been changed. Some had just recently been saved, and they all seemed so happy.

I was so enthused but pretty soon my brother Charlie grabbed me by the arm and said, "Come on, kid, you're going to the carnival. That's what we started out to do and that's what we're going to do!"

Believe me, I didn't enjoy a thing I saw or heard at that old carnival. All I could think of was that tent meeting across the street. As I think back, God must have been speaking to my young heart that night when we sat in the back seats and heard the old-time gospel preached for the first time. As we left the carnival grounds I said to Charlie, "That's the last carnival I'm ever going to. I mean it." And it was, glory to God.

I wanted to go back to that tent meeting so badly that my father, brother and sister finally took me. The preacher was a well-known woman preacher from St. Louis called Mother Barnes. She had been a Catholic until she was twenty-seven years old. Up until that time she had never touched a Bible and didn't know one verse in it. Then, one day, she went to a Methodist meeting where they had an altar call, and got saved. God called her to preach the gospel, and I really thank God that He did!

When she got to preaching and telling how God could save sinners, conviction came into our hearts, and daddy went forward to the altar. After he got saved, it didn't take long for me to follow. Six weeks later my sister was saved.

I was nothing but a child, but I knew from that time on my name was written in the Lamb's Book of Life. I had that peace within that I had been looking for so long. That old empty feeling was replaced with God's love.

In that same service God called me to preach the gospel. The Spirit of God was so great upon me He made me know that He called me. I was just so happy that God loved *me*, a little girl without a mother, with a vacant heart, and who knew nothing but hardship. When the Lord called me, I was so glad to go preach that I told Him I would go anytime, anywhere. And by His grace I have kept that promise. I didn't know a verse in the Bible, but I knew that something had happened to me far beyond words.

Walking home that night, I began to tell everybody I met how the Lord had saved me. My brothers and sisters were not saved and they were wondering what happened to me.

At first, I didn't tell anybody that God had called me to preach. I didn't think they would believe that the Lord would call a small, freckle-faced, stringy-haired girl like me. But God was faithful to His promise and began to use me. I'll never forget the first miracle I ever prayed for. One of our neighbors, Mrs. Williamson, who lived down the hill from us, was milking her cow one morning. The cow's calf had grown pretty big, but he wasn't weaned yet. When Mrs. Williamson tried to lead him away from his mother, he wouldn't budge. He wasn't ready to give up his breakfast yet. While she kept trying to lead him away, he got his foot on her foot, and she couldn't pull away. The harder she tried to pull or push him off, the more he twisted around on her foot. When she finally did get him off, her foot looked like it was almost pulverized. It swelled up to the size of a football, turned red, blue and green, and there were streaks running up her leg.

Mrs. Williamson had been going to the meetings with us, and the day of the accident she worried about missing the meeting. It was a mile or more, and we all had to walk, but somehow she managed to get there. The foot was all tied up, but she had brought along her shoe and stocking. Now that to me was real faith!

The service went on as usual, and after it was over people were just standing around talking. Some had gotten saved, and they were hugging each other and praising the Lord for what He had done that night.

I walked over to Mrs. Williamson and she told me what had happened. "Oh, that calf got on my foot and I don't know if it broke bones or not, but my foot is in awful shape." She unwrapped the bandage to show me, and then looked up and said, "Martha, do you believe God can heal my foot?"

"Oh," I replied, "I know He can!" There was no doubt at all. I just knew He could heal her foot. There were two or three other little kids standing around with me, and I told them, "We're going to pray for Mrs. Williamson's foot." Then I got down, laid my hands on her foot, and we prayed. When I got up and looked down at her foot again I saw it had gone down to normal size. The red streaks left right before our eyes. She put her stocking and shoe on and walked home with us, shouting all the way. What a thrilling experience!

Not long after I was saved I went on my first evangelistic trip with W.E. Hensel. Brother Hensel was one of the men saved in Mother Barnes's tent meeting, along with his wife and eight children.

A few weeks after Mother Barnes left town, Brother Hensel asked me and a lady named Rose Reif to come to his house. We stayed all night at their house, and the next morning Brother Hensel told us that the Lord had spoken to him about going someplace to be in a meeting. We asked him where, but he said he didn't know. I thought it sounded strange, but I still decided to go with them.

The ponies he used to pull his buggy were so wild, that we all had to go out and help him bridle them. He had a two seated surrey, and after hitching up the ponies, we all got in and started out. It was a hilly part of the country, and we only saw an occasional log cabin. The ponies were so wild, Brother Hensel looked like he was straining every muscle in his body just to keep them under control.

It was the fall of the year and the nights were cool. As it got on towards evening, Mrs. Hensel stopped and heated a rock to put in the buggy to help keep us warm. As we rode along we were singing at the top of our lungs. We sang all the songs we learned from Mother Barnes. Every so often I would ask, "Brother Hensel, do you know where we're going?" and he would just answer, "No, I don't, not yet."

That day we rode twenty-two-and-a-half miles, which wouldn't take long in a car, but in that little old buggy it seemed to take forever.

As it got darker and darker you could just see the old country road stretching out in front, and on either side the trees formed big black curtains. By this time I noticed Brother Hensel had tied the ponies' reins lightly to the front of the buggy, and was leaning back, letting them go where they would.

All at once the ponies turned off the main road and started

26

up a little road that seemed to head straight up the side of a mountain. No one was leading them, but they both turned at the same time, and up the side of the mountain we went. "Do you know yet where we're going?" I asked again. Brother Hensel replied, "No, but the Lord knows, and He's the one who's leading the ponies."

We got all the way to the top of that mountain and came to an old rail fence. The ponies trotted up to the fence and stopped. Brother Hensel looked over in the woods to the left and saw a little light through the trees. "I'll go over and see what it is. This may be where we're supposed to go." He went to check it out and in just a little bit returned. "This is it. There are three preachers down there holding a revival, and that's where God wants us."

At first I couldn't understand why we would be going there when there were already three preachers holding a meeting. But there was some prayer in back of this journey which we didn't know about. One of the preachers had a daughter named Fanny, who was a school teacher, and she had been praying for the revival.

We all got out of the buggy and went inside, walked up to the front row of the church and sat down. They were already singing so we started to sing just like the world was on fire. There weren't too many people, but our singing made a lot of difference and that place began to liven up.

Fanny asked Sister Rose and me to spend the night with her. We ended up staying for the whole series of meetings which lasted several days.

Along about the third day, the main preacher, whose name was Rev. Nicely, got up to preach. But suddenly he slammed his Bible down on the pulpit and said, "I'm not preaching another sermon until I get saved. Since these people, [meaning us] have come out here, I know that I'm not saved. I feel something different in their testimony and singing, and I know I don't have what they have.'' He asked if we would pray for him, and he got gloriously saved.

After the meetings ended, we returned home over those same winding roads, and were still several miles from home when it got dark. For some reason those wild ponies were more skittish than usual. They jumped at every little thing, and finally one broke loose altogether and ran off into the woods. We could hear him running through the woods and breaking down the underbrush. He was running big circles around the buggy. Brother Hensel began to pray and we all joined in. Brother Hensel just kept praying, and after a couple of hours, wonder of wonders, the pony came up and just stood there and let him put the harness back on. We then trotted off down the road as peaceful as you please.

This experience was really a great time of teaching for me, and in later years I remembered a lot of what happened on my first evangelistic trip. I learned a lot about what it meant to trust God and lean on Him in every situation.

The trip took place a short time after I was saved. A few days later God showed me definitely where I was to go and what I was to do. That God would show His will that way to a little motherless girl like me seemed unbelievable. But as I was praying upstairs in our little rented home there in West Plains, Missouri, the voice of the Lord spoke to me and said, ''Martha, go to the Oriental Hotel. Get a job, witness for Me, and preach the gospel until I bid you leave.''

People have asked me since then why daddy allowed me to go like that, but after he got saved he always felt that whatever the Lord was leading me to do was right.

My family was living out in the country at the time, and I had never set foot inside a hotel before. But I was so eager to do God's will that the following Saturday, I asked my sister Hattie to go with me to the Oriental Hotel as God had directed.

Hattie didn't like the idea. "Don't be foolish, Martha. You've never had any experience working in a hotel," she warned me. But I did know how to work because I had to do it at home. My sister was sick so much of the time that I was left with most of the work.

"Well," I said, "I know it sounds foolish, but will you go with me anyway?" She finally gave in, hitched up the horse and buggy, and drove me into town.

When we walked in that hotel, I felt real small and the place looked so scarey to me. We had to wait for some time in the lobby before Mrs. Summers, the woman who owned the hotel, finally came to talk to me. The longer we sat there, the more uneasy I felt but still I knew it was God's will.

Mrs. Summers finally arrived and asked, "What do you girls want?"

I straightened up and cleared my throat. "I want to get a job here," I answered.

"What do you know about working in a hotel?" she asked in what seemed to me a gruff voice.

"Ma'am, I've never been in a hotel before, and I know nothing about hotel work," I answered meekly. "But I can wash dishes, scrub the floor, and learn any kind of work you give me."

"We need a girl," she said in a slurring way, "but my husband is going out tomorrow to hire a girl who's had a lot of

29

experience. She's a big stout girl who knows all about the work.''

For her records she jotted down my name and address. I thanked her, and Hattie and I started for home.

The trip home wasn't very pleasant. All the way Hattie kept digging at me, "Now see what a fool you made of yourself, Martha? What made you think a little girl like you could get a job like that? You said the Lord told you to go there, so then why didn't you get it?''

"Well," I said, "all I know is the Lord told me to go there and get a job. I'll just leave it in His hands. He knows best.''

That was Saturday. The next day, I was shocked out of my shoes when a neighbor came running over to tell me there was a call for me. Phones were scarce in those days, and I had only talked on one once or twice. I couldn't imagine who it was.

I had to stand on my tiptoes to talk into the wall phone. "Hello, this is Martha Childers," I said in a clear voice.

"Martha, after you left, my husband and I talked it over.'' It was Mrs. Summers, the manager at the Oriental Hotel! "We decided we should hire you instead of the other girl. We were impressed that you'd be more reliable in the long run.''

I tried to say something, but the words wouldn't come. She continued, "My husband will be over in the morning to pick you up.''

"Yes, ma'am!'' was all I could say. God always gets the last laugh, I chuckled to myself as I hung up.

Mr. Summers came for me in the buggy about eleven o'clock the next day. My total belongings were packed in one big box and I left home never to return to my father's house to live again. Ever since that day I've been in the Lord's work, and I'm still following wherever He leads.

30

3

Because of my lack of experience, I had thought I'd be washing dishes, or cleaning rooms at the hotel. I had done a lot of that kind of work at home.

But when we got back to the hotel, Mrs. Summers said, "Martha, your room is upstairs. You'll stay with the other girls. Run up there now and brush up a bit. You're going to wait on tables." My heart skipped a beat! I didn't know a thing about waiting on tables at a hotel, but I knew the Lord was with me, so it worked out fine.

For an appetizer we always served a bowl of soup, and as I would lean over to place the bowl on the table, I would ask the person if he or she was a Christian. My mouth was just handy to their ears so I could speak right to them.

It was a new type of service, but that's the way I witnessed. Without hesitating, without picking out certain ones, I just asked everybody I could. There were many conversions in the almost two years I was there.

Some of the people I asked about being a Christian would

answer and say they belonged to such-and-such a church. "That's not enough," I would reply. "You have to know Christ and repent of your sins, too." It was effective because they thought it was so unusual for a little girl to be asking such a question. None of the customers ever bawled me out for asking, or speaking up like that. In fact some of them became so interested they came to the church I later pastored.

Not long after I got the job at the hotel, Rev. H.E. Bowley, the first pastor since I had gotten saved, came to town. God had called him to be a missionary to West Africa, so he didn't know how long he'd be able to pastor. Our congregation rented several different places for services, but finally we moved to a nice little church just about half a block up the street from the hotel on South Main Street. There were about two hundred people in the church all together.

Pastor Bowley only stayed about three or four months and then had to leave for Africa. That left the church without a pastor again, and we couldn't seem to find another one. There weren't any preachers around who preached the gospel or prayed for the sick.

When they couldn't seem to find a pastor, the people began to recognize the calling of God on my life. They asked me to become their pastor. I was only about thirteen years old at the time!

One night before Brother Bowley left, we had a meeting in which there seemed to be an odd feeling. Brother Bowley said there was a binding spirit. The next day we had another meeting in a private home, and in both meetings there was a preacher who wasn't living right. He belonged to one of the denominational churches, but he would come to the meetings at our church all the time. We had a lot of prayer and camp meetings.

In this afternoon meeting in a lady's home, Brother Bowley announced, "There was a binding spirit in the meeting last night." This backslidden preacher began to holler out and say, "It was me!" He talked about being demon-possessed, then he pulled out a knife and started to cut his own throat. And there I was just newly saved!

Brother Bowley said, "If anyone's afraid of a demon-possessed person, get out of the room." So everyone left except Brother Bowley, Sister Allan, the lady who owned the home, and myself.

The demon-possessed man jumped right up in the middle of the bed, and bent the iron bedsteads. All I could say was, "Well, God will give us power over the demon." So we prayed, and Brother Bowley rebuked and bound the devil, and the man got quiet.

While I was pastoring that first church, I continued to work at the hotel. It was a little hard to study the Bible when I had to work from five o'clock in the morning to late in the evening. Sometimes we would have an hour in the afternoon when we could rest or do some of our own things, and that's when I did my study. The church I was pastoring was an interdenominational church along the Apostolic line. Many people were saved and healed in that church, and it became the life of the city.

But unfortunately the people at the hotel were not in sympathy with my religious activities, and I was put to a real test. For two years the pressure was very great but I thank God that through it all I kept the victory.

On the day that Revelation 2:10 became my favorite verse, the people at the hotel deliberately gave me the hardest work to do. It was a pretty good-sized hotel, and they had lots of people checking in and out. On this particular day they decided they were going to make me give up my religion. They warned I would be in an asylum before I was twenty years old and that I would go crazy over religion.

That day they put me upstairs to do all the hard work. In those days they didn't have running water, and you had to carry all the big jars and pitchers up and down the steps. I had to refill all the pitchers with fresh water and carry them back up to the rooms. Those old pitchers were made of crockery and weighed a lot when they were filled with water. This was really a man's work, and they usually had a man do it.

I had to clean all the rooms too, and Mrs. Summers had said, "Don't just straighten the sheets, but pull them off and shake them first before putting them back on." Some of the beds looked like they had hardly been slept in, but I did as she told me. Every room I went in, I knelt down and asked God to put conviction on the people staying there and save them if they weren't already Christians. By the time I got to the second room the owners of the hotel were rejoicing because they thought all this hard work would really stop me from being a Christian.

Going into the third room, I knelt by the bed and prayed for the one who was staying in that room. I got up and was stooped over pulling sheets off the bed when a form came into the room. Now, my mother died when I was about eight months old, and I wouldn't know her if she walked right in before me, but the Spirit of God let me know that He had sent my mother in the form of an angel. She wore a snow-white dress, and had what looked like a bridal veil over the top of her head. Even her shoes were white and glittering. She walked over and laid her hand on my right shoulder and

34

called my name. She said, "Martha, be thou faithful unto death and Christ shall give thee a crown of life" (Rev. 2:10). That has been my favorite verse ever since.

After speaking those words, she just disappeared out of sight, like white smoke. As I continued to work, tears filled my eyes, tears of joy. In the midst of persecution, God had seen fit to give me one of the most beautiful experiences of my life. Even today I can almost feel that sweet touch of my mother's hand.

In addition to all the other work I had to do that day (I was also the head cook at this time and made all the biscuits, cakes, pies and special things), they sent the dishwasher home. Mrs. Summers told her to go home because Martha was going to do her work.

After the dining room closed around half past one or two in the afternoon, I had to clean up everything. While I was in the kitchen cleaning up all the pots and dishes, I said, "Lord, this is like heaven on earth. I can be all alone and talk to you." It was a wonderful experience and testimony at the same time.

An old man who came through the country every once in a while, came by real late that afternoon and asked Mrs. Summers if he could get a dinner.

"Certainly," she told him. She came into the kitchen and told me to kindle the fire and heat up everything for him. Instead of seating him by the door, she sat him down at the very last table at the end of our big, long dining room.

After loading my tray with food, I went through the swinging door and carried it back to him. When I put the tray down, I noticed he had tears in his eyes. He said, "Martha, if I ask you a question, will you answer it?"

"I will if I can," I said.

"When you came through that door, there was a light

shining all around you just like a rainbow, and it was so bright I could hardly look at it. What was that?''

I hardly knew what to say. ''That was the glory of God! Jesus is in my heart, and I feel His presence. It was His glory you saw.'' He just sat there and cried.

Then he asked me how my experience with Jesus came about.

''Well,'' I began, ''a year ago I went to an old-fashioned tent meeting. That was the first time I'd ever heard a woman preach. Her name was Mother Barnes, and she's come back this year and put her tent up on the same ground where I was saved. If you'll go down to that tent and ask God to forgive you of your sins, He'll save you just like He did me.''

That night, I wanted to go to the meeting so bad. I thought maybe he would go, and I could help him get to the altar. But I had to stay and wash all the supper dishes. It was real late when I got through with my night work, but I didn't stop praying for this man. Unfortunately, he left town, but later he sent word by one of the Christians to tell Martha at the Oriental Hotel that he had done what she said to do and gotten saved. He said it was my testimony that convinced him.

That had to be one of the hardest but happiest days of my life!

Several things stand out in my memory while I was pastoring the church there in West Plains. I grew real lonely to see Mother Barnes again and said, ''Oh, if I could just be close to her, just to feel that motherly touch of hers, it would be wonderful.''

Mother Barnes was holding meetings in a town about thirty miles from West Plains. One Sunday she came down and preached for us. As she was getting ready to leave after the services, she turned and waved her hand at me and said, "Martha, you'll be with Mother Barnes before long." At the time, I didn't understand what she meant.

I continued to pastor our church and one night just before the service, the wife and daughters of the backslidden preacher, the one who was demon-possessed, came to me and said, "Sister Martha, please pray. On the way to church, my husband threatened to kill us." She said he was determined to come that night and preach. When he came he walked right up on the platform and sat down. I was still just a little girl, and all I could do was pray.

This man's wife and daughters went over behind the old-fashioned organ and got down on their knees to pray.

In those days, we didn't have preaching until nine or after. First, there was always a testimony meeting. People would just enjoy telling what the Lord had done for them. Every once in a while, he'd pop up and say, "Well, you just keep on testifying if you want to, but I'm going to preach." I was praying, "Now, Lord, I'm not big enough to take care of this fellow, and I don't know what to do. If I order him out, he'll probably fight back and I'm just a little girl. Lord, you take him over."

Finally, everyone finished testifying, and he got up in the pulpit to preach. There was a bare electric light bulb that hung down right over the pulpit. This man had a large growth on the side of his neck, and because of it his head was always turned sideways. When he got up to preach, a big old bug that had been flying around the light flew right down into his ear!

He started hollering for his wife to come and get that bug out. The more he dug at it, the farther down it went inside his ear. Later, I heard they had to get the doctor to remove the bug from his ear. But that was the end of his preaching that night.

So I just thanked the Lord and went on preaching. God used ants, locusts, bees and all kinds of insects in the Bible, and that night He used that big old bug to answer my prayer.

I had been working at the hotel for some time when a lady who lived nearby took an interest in me. She owned a ladies' ready-to-wear and millinery store, and she asked me to work for her and learn the millinery trade. "I think it would be nice for you," she said. "You could go on with your preaching and singing at the same time you're learning here." Needless to say, I went to work for her.

After I worked there awhile, she decided the store would need a live model. No one had ever heard of having a live model before, not in those parts, because not many people had ready-made clothes.

I kept asking her where the live model was. "She'll be here when the time comes," she kept telling me. Finally, it was the night before we were to show a collection of beautiful new suits, hats, and dresses to the people. Everyone was just as anxious to see the live model as I was.

"Mrs. Stewart, we're getting close to the time. Where's the live model?" I asked.

Then she pointed her finger at me and said, "You, Martha, you're the live model!" I almost fell out of my chair. She put me in the store window to be the live model. I never had any fine clothes up until that time, but she had me wear everything from a housedress to a wedding dress. For several hours a day I had to stand in the window as still as possible.

I remember the first day I worked in the window. A little black boy came right up and mashed his nose against the window. I wasn't supposed to laugh or move, but he looked so funny, I was about to crack up. I started praying, "Lord, help me some way."

For the first time since I had been in there, the people started walking away. I could hear them saying, "Well, that's not a live person. She's run by electricity." Then I'd bat my eyes, and they would say, "They've got that down pat."

When these people all walked away, the little boy said real loud, "Can you walk?" I nodded my head, and he said, "Let's see you walk." I took a step or two. "Can you talk?"

I said, "I sure can, and you'd better scat right now!" By that time people were gathering again, and I'd gotten hold of myself.

Not long after I had started working there, there was an explosion and some wires short-circuited upstairs over the window where she dressed models. It caught fire and smoked real bad. She had to call in an auctioneer and hold a fire sale.

After the fire sale, the auctioneer's wife, whom I knew very well, came to me and said, "Will you come and live in our home?" They had an old-fashioned organ in the bedroom which I just loved, but after four days God had me moving on.

There was a man who lived next door and he told me, "Martha, you've worked so hard ever since you've been here. Your people have moved away, and now you need a rest. There's a short-term Bible school in Eureka Springs, Arkansas, that lasts four weeks. Would you like to go?"

Naturally, I wanted to go, but I had such a good home here. It was like heaven. The auctioneer's wife loved me like her own daughter and she had even told me I could take lessons on their old organ.

Finally I told Brother Cooper I would put out a fleece. "I'll pray about it, and if the Lord answers my prayer, I'll know whether to go or not."

I prayed, "Lord, if it's your will that I go, let me dream a dream that I'm there, talking to Mother Barnes. Let me see the place exactly as it is so I'll never doubt." I sure didn't want to make a mistake.

Then I went to bed and woke up at four o'clock in the morning without having dreamed a thing. I was so happy I could stay here in this lovely home, maybe for the rest of my life. But I went back to sleep again, and dreamed I was in Eureka Springs at a peculiar place where the houses were all built on top of one another. In this dream we went to a place called Chautauqua Hotel, a place I'd never heard of before. There was an old man who met people at the depot, and he met Mr. Cooper and me. He walked up and asked if we were coming to the Bible school. I told him we were and he said, "Well, they call me Uncle Jack. I take people from the depot to wherever they want to go, and I get them in touch with whomever they want to see."

"I want to go to the Chautauqua Hotel," I told him, "to be with Mother Barnes." Then in my dream we went up this particular mountain and into the hotel. When we entered the door, I noticed a counter with letters and papers on it and I asked Uncle Jack what that was.

"That's where they get their mail," he said. I walked up to the counter and asked if there was any mail for Martha Childers.

"I don't know," the clerk replied. "If you want any mail, you'll have to look through it yourself." I went through the stack of letters and pulled out two or three that were addressed to me. "Well, well. They wrote me even before I got here."

Then Uncle Jack said, "We'll go upstairs now to see Mother Barnes." He led us up a winding staircase. The hotel was dug right into the side of a mountain, and there were four or five stories. It was a great big place, and everywhere we looked there were singers, preachers, and gospel workers. When we got to the second floor, Uncle Jack knocked on a door and Mother Barnes opened it. "There's my Darling Child!" she said. (That was her favorite name for me.)

When I went in, she turned to a lady I had never seen and said to her, "Julia, just lay the cover back and let Martha lie down. She's tired from traveling all night. When she wakes up, you can bring dinner up to her." So I went to bed and slept.

When I woke up back in West Plains, I realized God wanted me to leave. It was sad to think I had to leave this nice home, but God was leading, and I left, never to return.

4

Everything in Eureka Springs turned out to be just exactly the way I had seen in my dream. Mother Barnes was wonderful, and treated me like I was her own child. One day she told me, "Martha, you're not going back to West Plains. You're going to travel with me and work for the Lord." And from then on, I traveled with her for five or six years before I married Brother Humbard.

In those days we had a lot of opposition. In fact, we still do, but I think people are not so open with it now as they were then. Some of the preachers in West Plains who didn't believe in divine healing or shouting once in a while got up a petition saying that Mother Barnes was a nuisance to the town. The pastor of the Christian Church was the ringleader, and these preachers with their petition had her arrested. They took her into court and accused her of disturbing the peace and of heresy.

She appeared before a man by the name of Judge Green, a friend of my father and a wonderful man. He liked Mother

Barnes's work and thought she was doing a great job getting all the drunks saved and their lives straightened out.

After all the preachers had testified against her, Judge Green asked Mother Barnes what she had to say for herself. She said she was only obeying God and seeing people delivered from the life of sin. The drunks were being delivered from sin and becoming good Christian citizens. Many had done as I did. They joined a church but were not saved because no one told them to repent, and never even prayed with them.

It seemed to her that some people didn't like her kind of preaching, but she told them she wasn't going to stop. They had hopes of putting her in jail, but she said if they did she would preach to the jailer. Nothing could stop Mother Barnes from preaching God's Word. It was kind of like pouring water on a duck's back. It just keeps running off!

While helping Mother Barnes in Eureka Springs, and traveling with the group, I also managed to attend school. One Saturday I was looking out the window when I saw a wagon parked across from the school. It belonged to a man and his nine-year-old son who had come to Eureka Springs to bring a wagon load of turnips to sell. The man lived out on a farm fifteen miles from town, and after selling all his turnips he had parked the wagon and mules right down in front of the school.

While I was staring at that wagon, the Lord spoke to me, "Get in that wagon. I've got something for you to do." Well, that was strange because I had never seen that man before. I looked around and saw my friend, Mary Krauss, coming down the hill. She and I had been singing and working together for the Lord. "Sister Mary, the Lord has told me to get in that wagon down there and go somewhere." It sounded awfully silly, but I just knew it was the Lord.

"If you go I'm going with you," said Mary. We knew one girl who lived out that way about five miles, but we didn't think she had anything to do with it. So we got ready to go. I only had about fifteen cents while Mary didn't have any money.

We got in the wagon, but neither the man nor his son were around. There were two mules tied to the back of the wagon, and all we could do was climb on the back of the wagon and sit there. When the man and his son finally came, the only thing the man said to us was "Would you girls lead these mules?" So there we were, leading a team of mules and not knowing where we were going. You might say this was a foolish thing to do, but then they thought Abraham was foolish too.

That morning there had been a real hard rain and in the Ozark Mountains the creeks and rivers fill pretty fast. We had to cross the Beaver River which was up very high by then. They had a man on horseback watching the river, and he hollered at us not to try to ford it because there wasn't any bridge. We had to wait two or three hours until the water receded so we could get across.

Finally, the man gave the signal and let us through. I began to think we weren't going to make it. The river was still so high on the wagon that I could reach out my hand and touch the water. But we made it across the river just fine. (Fortunately the river bottom was solid rock.)

Mary kept asking me, "Do you know where we are going yet?"

"No," I kept answering, "I don't know any more where

45

we're going than you do, but I know God is in it, so let's just follow the Lord."

After a good while we saw a light in a house, and we drove up to this beautiful country home. When the man got out of the wagon he didn't say anything. He didn't know who we were, and he had never asked us where we were going or anything. The only time he had spoken to us at all was when he asked us to lead the mules. As he got out of the wagon, Sister Mary said to me, "Well, what are we going to do?"

"We're going to get out and follow him," I insisted.

After jolting over that rocky road for so long, I felt like I could have eaten anything, even raw potatoes. So we walked up to the door behind this man and all he said to his wife was "I don't know who these girls are." (I felt kind of sorry for him in a way having to explain our presence.) But his wife was very nice, and told us to come in.

"I'm starving to death!" Mary whispered to me. I was hungry too. (If you've ever tried jolting over fifteen miles of rocky Ozark Mountain trails, not having much to eat before you started, you'll know what it's like.)

Just then she said, "I guess you folks are hungry, would you like to have something to eat?" My, was I glad to hear her say that!

"Yes ma'am, if you have something."

"I'll just kindle up a fire and cook you something."

"Just anything left over from dinner will do, something cold is all right." I could have eaten anything and I knew Mary could too. So she took a beautiful white linen cover off the table and underneath it the table was full of food left from dinner. There were boiled vegetables and lots of good country butter.

"I have plenty of milk. Do you like milk?" she asked.

46

Now I could drink a quart of milk most any day at a meal. "Yes, ma'am, I'd sure like milk."

When we got through, she said "If you girls don't mind I'll fix you a bed upstairs." I was thrilled because now I could pray and find out what this was all about.

As we got into bed I said to Mary, "Now when we hear her get up in the morning, we'll get up with her."

Bright and early the next morning we heard her and right away I got up and made the bed. She fixed us a nice breakfast, and when we were through she said, "I've got to go now and milk the cows." While she was gone, we washed the dishes and had them all washed and dried by the time she got back. It was about eight or half past and she asked, "Would you girls like to go to church? We don't have a regular pastor or preacher, but we'd like to have you girls go to church if you'd care to."

I said, "Yes, we'd sure like to go with you." We didn't tell her we were gospel workers and singers. Mary didn't preach at the time but I did. So we all walked across the pasture and up the hill to this little country church she called Oak Hill.

Once inside they asked if either of us could play the organ. I spoke up and said Mary could. So they asked her to play for them, and I guess by the way we sang and played they could tell we had some experience. An older man got up and said, "I presume [I didn't know what the word 'presume' meant] that these girls are some kind of gospel workers, or singers or something. In that case, would you sing us some special songs?"

So we sang and they enjoyed it very much.

After a while, he "presumed" again. "Do you girls happen to be some kind of gospel workers or something?"

Before you could say "scat," Mary answered "Sister Martha preaches." Well, that started things off. They asked us if we could have a service for them that night and we agreed. They called everyone around that hadn't been there in the morning and the place was packed. It was cold out, and they had a big heater in the middle of the church. The stove pipe was suspended from the ceiling by wires, and the stove pipe came clear back over the platform.

That night as I made the altar call, a number of people came down for salvation. There was one boy, I'd judge him to be about twelve or thirteen years old, with big brown eyes and brown hair. He had such a beautiful countenance, his face seemed to just light up with the glory of God. His name was Rex Wright, and incidentally, that's where I got Rex's name. I had never heard of anyone with that name before, and I commented to Mary, "If I ever marry and have a son his name is going to be Rex."

Those folks were so pleased they asked us to stay on and hold a revival, and we stayed on many more nights. It was wonderful because there were so many souls that were saved in that little country church.

But they had never told us that every revival in the past had always been disrupted by a bunch of fanatics. These people lived about eleven miles away, and they would come in whenever they heard there was a revival going on. When the service would start getting good, these people would get up and start bouncing around and falling over the pews. Then the mothers with children would get up and get out of there before their children would get hurt. It seemed like nobody could stop these fanatics either.

One night during our revival these people came and sat down right in the front row. The meeting was going on, and I had started to preach when all of a sudden a big man jumped up. He swung his feet and legs out, and began to run up and down the aisles. People began to grab their children and get ready to leave. Then this fellow bumped up against that hot stove, and hit it so hard he almost knocked the stove pipe out of it. I bowed my head and prayed, "Lord, you bring that guy up here and let him fall right in front of me. I know what he's doing is not of you, but of the devil."

Now I don't claim to have the gift of discernment or anything, but I just knew what he was doing was not of God. Well, I hardly got done praying when he came running up that aisle and fell right in front of me. I got down on my knees and put my mouth down pretty close to his face and said, "What you're doing is of the devil. You're trying to break up this revival, but you're not going to do it. I bind the devil in you in the name of Jesus. Now you get up from there and get over on that seat and sit down. If you don't, I'll take you by the collar and see that you do sit down!"

After the meeting people came up and told me how they could never have revivals before because of these people carrying on. One old man came up crying and said, "I thank God for you, Sister Martha. You're the first evangelist who's ever come here and been able to stop them."

There was always something exciting happening during the years I traveled with Mother Barnes. Once we were in Springfield, Missouri, with a big tent that seated about 1,250 people. Even at that it couldn't hold all the people that came. They'd line up out on the sidewalk and all around the tent.

One Sunday afternoon, Mother Barnes told me, "Darling

Child, you lead the testimony service this afternoon." As I was leading the testimony service, I began to talk in a language I didn't know. I wasn't really feeling anything different; no frenzy, no shaking, just talking. I was just standing there talking and listening to myself. It was real enough, but I didn't know a word I was saying. Then suddenly I quit speaking in that language and went on leading the testimony service. People were getting up and thanking God for the tent meeting, telling how God had healed them of different diseases.

When Mother Barnes gave the altar call, she told us workers to get down by the altar bench and be ready to pray with the unsaved. So I was standing by the altar bench when a well-dressed woman with beautiful black eyes and black hair came up to me with tears flowing down her cheeks. She said, "Little girl, you speak my language." I told her I didn't know what she was talking about. "But you do," she insisted "How did you know my name?"

"Ma'am, I never saw you before!" But she just kept insisting that I spoke her language. I told her I couldn't even speak my own language too well, and I certainly didn't speak any other.

She kept on, "Well, then how did you know where I lived?"

"I don't know where you live!" I replied.

"But you know my house number!"

"Ma'am, I only know two streets in Springfield, one of them is St. Louis Street which runs into the square, and the other one is Booneville."

She looked very puzzled, "But you talked plainly in my language, and you told me my sins. You told me not to confess my sins to a man, but to God. You told me to come to

50

Jesus Christ and confess my sins, that this was my time to get right with God." Suddenly I began to wake up to the fact that God had spoken directly through me. I will never forget that woman's look as she spoke with me. The tears were just pouring from her eyes. "You told me things that no one knew but me and God."

"Ma'am, that was the Holy Ghost speaking through lips of clay, directly to you," I explained. "God sure loves you, and you'd better obey whatever He told you to do. I don't know what He said."

When I told her that it was the Holy Ghost, God's Spirit speaking to her, and that He loved her, she fell on the altar like she'd been shot. I got down beside her, and she confessed her sins and gave her heart to God.

Even in hard times God was with me and worked miraculously. One summer I was visiting my sister and her husband in Springfield, Missouri. They had a large restaurant on St. Louis Street. One morning I had a deep burden on my heart to pray so I stayed in my room. When I got through praying, I felt led to write my father a letter. I only had one piece of paper and one envelope, but I didn't have a stamp or even the two cents to buy one. I didn't tell my sister because the Lord spoke to me in prayer right after I was saved and said, "Don't ask your father, brother, or sisters or any of your kin for anything, not even a penny. I will supply your needs." So I would never ask anyone for anything. I got my letter all written and the envelope addressed and by faith I walked down towards the mailbox.

Now I was in a big, strange city and it was several blocks to the mailbox. The street was pretty crowded with people, in fact, it was so crowded that people were bumping into each other. There I was, just a little girl walking along with my letter, holding it to my heart and talking to the Lord. "Lord, I'll mail this by faith, even though it doesn't have a stamp on it."

All at once in that big crowd a fine-looking lady (I thought she was a millionaire) just pushed her way through the crowd right in front of me. So I stepped aside to get around her, and she stepped in front of me again. I stepped the other way but she followed me. I stopped to let her go around me, but she stopped and said, "What have you been doing today?" She had such a sweet voice, that I've wondered lots of times since then if she was one of God's angels. I hardly knew what to say to this stranger.

"Writing a letter, for one thing," I replied.

"Oh, that's what I've been doing. Where are you going now?"

"I'm going to the mailbox up there on the corner by the Woodruff building."

Then without further explanation she reached over and pulled the corner of my envelope down. "Well, you don't even have a stamp on your letter, do you?"

"No, ma'am, I don't."

"Here, I have an extra one. Would you like to have it?"

"Ma'am, I don't have two cents to pay for it."

"I don't want you to pay for it." With that she licked the stamp and put it on my letter. I didn't even have to lick the stamp! That was a real boost to my faith. If that wasn't from the Lord, I don't know what was. I guess that's how God keeps me going. Things that look impossible are easily done by Him.

5

My father remarried again after I left home. I had not spent a summer at home with my father since leaving to work at the Oriental Hotel. One summer a friend, Catharine Sutherland, and I made plans to spend a nice, quiet vacation at home with my father. I had built her up for the big event by telling her how we would have such a wonderful time praying and reading the Bible, and how it would be so nice just to rest. Catharine was a teacher at Mother Barnes's Ozark Bible and Literary School in Eureka Springs. She and I sang a lot together at the school, and we planned to do a lot of practicing during our vacation.

On the day of our arrival my father met us at the railroad station with an old road wagon and a team of mules. We loaded our things and got up in the spring seat. My father said, "Well, we'd better hurry home and get ready. We're going to have a service tonight."

"Papa, where are you going to have a service?" I asked. He just laughed and said that we had a good place for a revival and that I was going to be real surprised. That's all he'd say the rest of the way.

When we got near enough to see the house, it looked very strange. My little old-fashioned organ I'd bought before was setting on the front porch and the yard was full of wooden plank seats. "Now what's this?" I pondered.

"This is where we're going to have the revival, right here in our own front yard," he smiled proudly. It seemed awfully strange to me, but sure enough, that night we had a good revival right there in our front yard.

A second revival was begun three miles from my father's home under an old-fashioned brush arbor. For those who can't remember back that far, a brush arbor was made by stringing poles or wires between tree limbs, and then covering them with cut branches to form a covering.

This second revival started on the first of July, and on the second day I passed out with a hard chill. I had been in services every night except two for two whole years, and I guess my body was pretty run-down.

Fortunately, my stepmother was a trained nurse, and she instantly recognized my symptoms as typhoid fever. From the very first, she claimed my body was too run-down and there was no hope of me living through it.

My friend Catharine Sutherland also knew that there was no hope for me outside of the Lord. I was right at death's door but the strange thing is that, through it all, I knew everything that was going on. I could hear them whispering very plainly, but they didn't know I knew a thing. I got so close to heaven, or so it seemed, that I could hear a little heavenly music. With all this, I was anxious to go on and be with the Lord. And since I couldn't go on with the revival, they sent for another evangelist, Rev. Frank Anderson of Texas.

They couldn't get my fever down, it just stayed up real high. In the meantime they packed me in cold packs and did everything possible. But it just wasn't enough.

One night I got so bad Catharine thought I was dying. She got right up and took me in her arms just like I was a baby and begged God to let me live. I believe she was the one who prayed the prayer of faith for me. She just kept praying, "Please, God, let Martha live. Please don't let her die!" The others had already given me up to die, for they thought I couldn't possibly live.

Well, I lingered through the night and went through a strange experience. In the night it seemed to be that the Lord spoke to me and said, "Would you be willing to stay here if you could see souls saved?"

I hesitated. I really didn't want to say yes, because I knew I was saved and ready to go. Finally I said in my weak way, "Lord, I'm willing to stay if I can win souls, if that's your will. But I'd rather go on and be with you and my mother and the loved ones that have gone on."

So the Lord brought me clear down to where He said, "Would you be willing if only one soul was saved?"

I knew that one soul is worth more than the whole world. Finally I said, "Lord, if that's your will, I'll go or stay. It doesn't matter to me. I'd rather go, but if it's your will I stay to help some soul find you, I'm willing."

The next day, about half past three in the afternoon, I heard my stepmother say, "Catharine, I've got to get out if this room. I've been here so long." So she went out to a little garden by the back yard gate and told the others she was going out to pick some vegetables and get her mind on something else. "If there's any change, call me," she instructed.

She had just begun to pick a few beans, when the power of God seemed to strike me and go all through my body, from the top of my head to the soles of my feet. The burning hot fever completely disappeared and I never felt better in my life. I sat up in bed and said, "Catharine, I'm healed! Jesus Christ has healed me! I'm healed! I'm healed!" I guess she thought I was delirious because I jumped out of bed and began to praise the Lord.

By that time, my stepmother heard the commotion and rushed in. She told Catharine, "She doesn't know what she's saying. I've nursed this kind for years. She's going from better to worse."

"No, mamma, Jesus Christ has healed me. I'm well!" I insisted.

But she didn't believe me. Instead she got me by my left arm, and Catharine got me by the right and they both tried to get me back to bed. "She's delirious and doesn't know a thing she's saying. She'll be gone in a little while!" my stepmother warned.

I said, "No, you are not getting me back into that bed. Jesus Christ has healed me!"

Even though Catharine had held me and prayed in faith the night before, she seemed to agree with my stepmother, who kept insisting I was delirious.

I usually couldn't remember the name of Catharine's hometown in Canada, so Catharine said, "Do you know who I am?"

"Why, of course I do. You're Catharine Sutherland."

"She's got that right! What's my hometown?"

56

For the first time I remembered and said, "Glencoe, Ontario, Canada." With that she began to believe I was really healed.

All those days I had had nothing to eat or drink but cold water and buttermilk, so I was starving. I said to Catharine, "Get my clothing, draw me some bath water, and put it in the side room. I'm going to have a bath and then eat. I'm starved! I want you to call everybody on the telephone line and tell them we'll be having a service tonight!"

Catharine got the water ready, and I took my own bath, dressed myself, and went in to eat supper.

My stepmother began crying, "This will kill her. She can't eat like this!" Even my own daddy's faith seemed to be slipping. "Don't you think you ought to go a little light?" he pleaded.

"No, daddy, I don't." When I went to the table I had to throw all my manners away. They were all hollering; "Don't take this, don't eat that, you can't! Don't you realize you're weak? You're sick! This will kill you!"

There were big slabs of hickory-smoked ham, a big bowl of sauerkraut, homemade light bread, pickles and all kinds of vegetables. My stepmother could really cook. The table was piled with food. I got my fork in one hand and jabbed it into the largest piece of ham I could find. I knew I wouldn't have time to dip the kraut, because they wouldn't let me have kraut if they could stop me, so I just tipped the bowl and poured it on my plate. They would have been happy enough to allow me just a little buttermilk, but I was so hungry I just piled the food on my plate and started grabbing.

All the while my stepmother was over by the old cook stove bawling, "I know she'll die if she eats that. If the fever

57

doesn't come back and kill her, surely that meal will.''

''Mamma, Jesus Christ has healed me and I can eat anything. Catharine, go to the neighbors and call everybody on the line and tell them I'll be at the brush arbor tonight to speak.'' She called and heard all the receivers coming up, click, click, click. Everybody in the neighborhood was on a party line, and every time anybody called they expected to hear I was dead.

When I finally got up from the table, I said, ''Let's hurry up and get to the meeting.''

''You're not going to that meeting,'' they shouted.

''I sure am! Catharine announced on the phone that I'd be there to preach!'' That night I rode three miles in a road wagon to preach, and if that isn't a miracle, I don't know what is.

I don't know where all the people came from, but when we got to that brush arbor there was a big crowd. The news had spread that God had healed me from typhoid fever, and people came from as far away as Jonesboro.

I spoke in that meeting to all those people, some of whom had known me for years. They all came to see this wonderful miracle, and I'll never forget the wonderful power and presence of God.

It had quite an effect on my stepmother. Before the miracle she always said it wasn't any use to pray out loud and make noise. When Catharine and I prayed, we would go way down in the pasture, because we believed in shoutin' a little. Mamma would say, ''It's no use going way down there. I can still hear you.'' So we had our prayer in the living room. Each morning we went in there to pray after I was healed. My daddy was there, and to my surprise, my stepmother came in and knelt down. "I want the kind of religion that you and pappy's got," she confessed. So we prayed with her and she got saved two days after my healing.

After Mamma got saved, I said, "Oh Mamma, won't it be wonderful? Next Sunday we're going to have a baptism in the creek!" (We had to cross the creek every night on the way to the brush arbor meeting.) "You can be baptized with all the new converts."

"No waiting till next Sunday for me! I'm going to be baptized on my way to church tonight! I might die before next Sunday, or Jesus might come," she declared. So we left a little early for church and stopped at the old creek to baptize her. My little half brother Gene who had just gotten saved was baptized at the same time. I'll tell you, when that stepmother of mine got baptized, she began waving her hands and having a jubilee. She said she hadn't known it was so wonderful to know Christ like that, and here she had never read the Bible, and she didn't know what was in it.

We stayed there with my father and stepmother all summer. That was the longest time I ever spent in my father's home at one time after I started working for the Lord, but there were to be many other visits.

On another visit back to my father's farm, I brought some other girls along. There were singers and a couple of lady preachers, Winnie Webster and Mildred Sample.

We went to where my father lived near Jonesboro, and found that daddy had built a brush arbor and wanted to have some meetings while we were there.

We had just started the meeting one evening, and I had just gotten up to preach when a woman came running up to me. "Come quick, it's serious!" she cried. I didn't have any idea

59

of what it was, but I followed her instantly. When we got outside the arbor, the lady said, ''My husband and stepson have been on the outs. It's a serious thing and it's come to a climax tonight. They both have said they're going to kill or get killed.''

Their house was less than half a block from the brush arbor, and she felt certain there was going to be trouble. As she spoke the burden fell on my heart, and I began to travail in the Spirit for them. The burden got heavier, and I began to pray and cry. Words just couldn't be uttered. When I reached the front porch, I fell down on the ground with loud groans. Her husband came up about that time and wanted to know what was wrong with me.

''Sister Martha has a burden!'' his wife said.

They picked me up, carried me into the house, and laid me on the bed. I was just groaning like I would die. My whole soul and body seemed like it was crying out to God for these two souls. As I lay there groaning, the man again asked his wife, ''What's the matter with her?''

''She has a heavy burden on her heart.''

''Well, who for? What's it all about?''

''If you must know, it's for you!''

When he heard that, tears came to his eyes. In spite of my state, I could still hear them talking. Then wonder of wonders, as I lay there groaning and crying for these two, in walked the son. It looked like the climax had come right there in front of me!

He said ''What's the matter with Sister Martha?''

''She has an awful burden for someone,'' his mother replied.

''Who?''

"For you!" She pointed an accusing finger.

Both of those men stood there with tears, and I just kept groaning and crying out to God until they all at once reached out and clasped each other's hand. They both asked forgiveness, and as soon as they had done that my burden lifted. I could talk again and everything. Oh, my, I sure know what God meant when he talked about "Zion travailing." I really felt that if something hadn't been done about changing their lives, that that would have been the end of my life.

Mother Barnes would sometimes call me in and ask me to pray with her for backsliders. One time it was really a big backslider, a preacher who had become ensnared in a relationship with someone who wasn't his own wife. Mother Barnes called me in and said, "Darling Child, come in and help pray for this backslider." I didn't know why they backslid or what they had done, but I prayed anyhow. When we would pray, and they got back to the Lord, they seemed so happy.

"I thought, "Oh, it must be wonderful to be a backslider." If you don't know all the Bible says, then it's easy to get the wrong idea about some things. I was starting to study the Bible, but I hadn't heard about backsliding yet. One day I got up enough nerve and asked Mother Barnes about it. I just walked into her living room and said "Mother Barnes, why don't I backslide?" I was really serious about the thing. I thought it was something really wonderful to see those backsliders get back; they really seemed happy when they did. I thought that was another blessing, and I sure didn't want to miss any blessings that the Lord might have for me.

Well, Mother Barnes just laughed and held her sides. I don't know what she must have thought at first. She just laughed and laughed. Finally, she calmed down and said, "Well, Darling Child, you're too busy to backslide. Nobody backslides except people who are careless and lazy and won't get out and work for the Lord, and won't testify for God. They just quit praying and going to church and living right. That's a backslider!" After she explained what it was I didn't want to be one.

She wanted to know why I had asked that question. I just told her it seemed like they got such a blessing when we prayed for them, that I thought maybe it would be another good blessing I could get.

At the Ozark Bible and Literary School, the rooms were arranged so that four girls shared two adjoining rooms with a door between. There were four of us in the two rooms where I lived. Two of them were school teachers there at the school. We named our apartment the Best Joy Bell apartment, because one of the girls was Kathryn Best, another Janet Joy, the third Lillian Bell, and myself, Martha Bell.

One day my roommates and I were going to do the laundry. It was quite a load because it included not only our own and Mother Barnes's but the linens from the guest rooms and the scarves from the prayer tower as well. We had gotten up at five in the morning since we didn't have a washing machine and would have to use the washboard. The laundry took so long that we missed the 9:30 service. But we did finish in time to go downtown to the big mission hall for the eleven o'clock service.

They were having a big convention and there were a lot of preachers in town participating in the meeting. We came in late and found some seats around the middle of the auditorium and sat down. The platform was filled with preachers, but there was one preacher there whom my eyes seemed to fasten on. I had never seen him before, but there was a love in my heart for this particular preacher, though I didn't know why. I had never met him, never seen him before, but I knew I'd never forget him either!

After the service everyone was shaking hands, so I met him and shook his hand. In return he gave me a little tract he had written entitled "Jesus, Our Only Hope." His picture was on the front. It also had his name and address. I could have written him, but I wasn't the flirting kind. Right after meeting him the convention closed and all the preachers left. I never got acquainted with him, in fact I never even talked to him. But I did cut the picture off the front of his tract and paste it on the back of a snapshot album. (It's still there today, just as bright as ever.)

One afternoon just before the convention ended, I was in the parlor practicing the piano. The rules were that when any of the students were in the parlor practicing, no one was allowed to disturb you. But all at once the door opened and in walked a preacher. (He wasn't the same one I had seen on the platform.) He walked up to the piano, and I looked up to see who had disobeyed the rules. He came up to me and said, "I understand that you are one of Mother Barnes's workers."

"Yes, sir, I travel, and work here at the school with her," I replied.

"I also understand that you're a minister," he went on. "Yes, I am."

"Then would you write and tell me about this school?"

Now I was always busy, as help was scarce, and this was a relatively new place, but I told him I supposed I could. So the very next day I got a letter from him. I think he must have written the letter before he left town, because it was postmarked Eureka Springs. It was almost a love letter, and he continued writing for several months. I wrote him back, but never a love letter or anything like that. He kept it up and over the months we got engaged just writing. We had never gone out, and I had never been with him.

In one of his letters he said, "Now you're a Gospel worker, and I am too, so I don't know why it wouldn't be God's will for us to get married." He kept writing like that, and finally I told him I would marry him.

We were holding some meetings in Arkansas at the time and I was doing most of the preaching since Mother Barnes was getting old and wasn't well that summer. One day she called me in and said "Darling Child, it's just too hard for you to do all of the preaching." (We had three services a day.) "I'm going to get a preacher to come and help with the work." To my surprise, she got this preacher I was engaged to. He helped us in the revival about midway between Hoxie and Walnut Ridge, Arkansas. A big church was established there and still exists as a result of that revival.

After leaving there we went to Seligman, Missouri, for our next tent meeting. This young preacher was twenty-two years old, had meetings set up in Louisiana and Texas for later in the month. One day before he left Seligman, I was in the big combination dining room and kitchen that we had rented. I always cooked the dinner for the band of workers which numbered twenty to twenty-five people. We didn't have room in the house for all of the workers, and some of them had cots in the tent. We also had a cot in the kitchen. This preacher I was engaged to was lying on the cot over in the corner of the kitchen while I cooked dinner. Then all at once God spoke to me. "This boy, this preacher, is not the one for you."

Almost immediately, one of the girls came running down the stairs to the kitchen and said to me, "Mother Barnes wants you at once."

I was peeling potatoes, but I dropped everything and ran upstairs. I thought to myself, "While I'm up there, I'll tell her what God said to me about this preacher."

But as soon as I walked in the door, she said, "God has spoken to me that this preacher is not the one for you to marry."

"God has spoken the same thing to me!" I exclaimed with relief.

But I didn't tell him right away because I was afraid it would interfere with the meetings we were holding there in Seligman. I waited until he left and then wrote and told him what the Lord had said. He had a hard time accepting it, and just couldn't see why it wasn't the Lord's will for us to marry.

A month later we were getting ready for a big camp meeting to be held in Eureka Springs. Mother Barnes told me she was going to leave me there in Seligman. "We have a real work started here and you'll have to stay here and pastor" she explained. We'd had probably a hundred or two hundred people saved and no place to worship.

"If that's what you want me to do, I'll stay and pastor your work until you get somebody else," I promised her. I was perfectly willing and so the day came when they were scheduled to leave. It was sixteen miles from Seligman, Missouri to Eureka Springs, Arkansas. Everyone was all packed and ready to go when Mother Barnes came to me and said that God had spoken to her and had said to take me along. I stopped what I was doing and started packing. This was at four o'clock, and I was finished packing and we were on our way by six o'clock. We did all of our traveling by train in those days.

We got back to Eureka Springs and in a day or two the meetings began. The first meeting was starting when I looked up on the platform and spotted the preacher from the previous year standing up there between two preachers. As soon as I saw him, I realized I had had love in my heart for him all this time. I hadn't known if I would ever see him again, and he didn't even know my name. All I had was his picture from the tract he had given me. Later he told me he was in love with me, but couldn't write me because he didn't know my name. After the camp meeting closed, the preachers were all packed and ready to go. We had an early dinner for them that day because the train left Eureka Springs around 11 A.M. Now this preacher who was in love with me, Alpha Humbard, was all packed and still hadn't gotten a chance to talk to me. Everybody began to shake hands and say good-bye, and finally he came over to shake my hand.

"I understand you're one of the workers that helped Mother Barnes in that great meeting between Hoxie and Walnut Ridge," he said.

"Yes, sir, I was."

"Could you give me the names of some of the people who live there? I'm thinking about going there for a revival." I gave him several names of people. He thanked me and took the paper, then handed it back to me. "Would you put down your name and address too?" I agreed, and that was how he found out my name. When he got down to the train depot, he decided he just couldn't leave me like that, so he came back to the school. Now the school was so big he could have been there three days and not seen me, but I just happened to be waiting on the guest table in the back corner of the dining room. It faced the door that opened out on the porch which ran from one end of the building to the other. All at once, while I was cleaning a table off, I saw a hand holding a light-colored hat. I threw everything down and went running to the porch and the door that led into the lobby. I reached the door (by then I had slowed down) and started to walk. He was standing in the lobby, leaning up against the counter.

I had some questions I wanted to ask him about the baptism of the Holy Ghost, for he taught a little differently from a lot of preachers. When I saw him I said, "I wanted to ask you some questions on the Bible, but I didn't have the chance.

"I can only give you the Word of God" he answered, and then proceeded to give me the Scriptures he had been teaching from. "God sent you in here," he said as we finished. I wondered how he knew that God had sent me, but I felt it too. He left the room then and I went back to clean up the tables and finish my work.

We had an old-fashioned organ sitting in the corner of the dining room, and when I finished my work I sat down and began to practice one of my favorite songs, "I'm Going There Some Day." I'd been practicing it on the piano, so I thought I'd try it on the organ. As I was practicing, a couple of preachers walked back and one of them was Brother Humbard.

"Can I talk to you?"

"Yes, sir," I answered, still a bit puzzled by his

reappearance. The big thing I found out about Brother Humbard was he didn't have anything in his life to cover up. I think he told me his whole life story up to the present, and there didn't seem to be anything he didn't want me to know. He just opened up his precious heart and told me what the Lord had spoken to him. "I don't know how you feel about this, but God spoke to me about you the first time I ever saw you. God said, 'You have been faithful to me, and haven't sought a wife, but if you want a helpmate who will stand true to you through life and death, there she is in the middle.' " (I had walked into the auditorium the first time he saw me between my two roommates.)

At first he had been afraid it was the "old enemy" trying to tempt him. He had thought he might never marry, but only serve the Lord, and I had thought the same thing about myself.

Well, when he told me all this, I said, "Maybe the Lord is in this. I'll pray about it." We both earnestly prayed because we didn't want to be hasty.

After our long conversation, Brother Humbard went to Webb City, Missouri, to hold a meeting, and he wrote me his first letter. I still have the letter and sometimes I take it out and read it over. He wrote, "Dear Sister in Christ, Peace be unto you! You have my heart and I cannot help it!"

Mary Krauss and I in Carrollton, Illinois. We traveled one summer for Mother Barnes.

One time we had car trouble and almost didn't make it back for the night meeting. Mother Barnes is at the center of the picture and I am to her right.

Housecleaning day at the school in Eureka Springs. We tried to get Bro. Humbard (*right*) to join us. That's me in the white hat up front.

I had this picture taken while I was working at the Oriental Hotel.

Here I am with two friends. Ida (*right*) worked with me at the Oriental Hotel.

Rex at age fifteen practicing his
guitar which he has been playing
since he was a small boy.

Clement has a natural gift for music.
Here he plays the banjo,
one of his many instruments.

This is the Gospel Temple right after we moved in. The first revival lasted two years and ten months, seven days a week.

This is me in 1935 with my Bible and guitar in front of the Gospel Temple.

My father and his cousin, Nellie, whom he visited in Bedford, Indiana.

Bro. Humbard and I during the days when we were at the peak of our ministry together in Hot Springs, Arkansas.

The Humbard family: Bro. Humbard, Rex, Ruth (*holding Mary*), Leona (*holding Juanita*), Clement and I.

This was taken in 1912,
the year after I was saved.

Clement and Priscilla and their lovely family: Rebecca, Delilah, and the
twins, Drucilla and Suzanne.

This was taken sometime in the sixties when we were still at Hot Springs.

This is the picture I use for newspapers when out on my evangelistic meetings. I'd rather "refire" than "retire." I've got to keep going for my Lord.

An early picture of Juanita,
our youngest.

Ruth and Lewis Davidson, the pastor of Calvary Temple, in Parma, Ohio.

Leona and Wayne Jones and their children Bob, Ronnie and J. Harold in a family portrait taken in 1965. (Buddy was away at college when this picture was taken.)

This is Mother Barnes whose preaching led me to the Lord and then into a lifetime of service for him.

The Humbard family. Back row: Rex, Leona, Dad, Mom, Clement. Front row: Mary, Ruth, Juanita.

Rex and Maude Aimee with their two oldest, Rex, Jr. and Don.

The Cathedral of Tomorrow.

Rex Humbard and Mom Humbard.

6

Our meetings were going real good in Carrollton, Illinois, but it got too cold to hold the meetings in the tent. A man in town who owned a big dance hall came to me and said, "Little Martha, as long as you and Sister Mary [Mary Krauss] play and sing together so well, I'll give you a place to hold your meetings in. You can stay there as long as you want without paying a penny." It was really a beautiful place he had, and it included pianos and organs and hot and cold running water. But meanwhile the influenza had broken out, and we were in that building for only four nights when we were notified that all public meetings were closed down because of the epidemic.

I was still in charge of the band of workers as Mother Barnes was off having meetings in other places. I didn't know what to do so I began to pray for direction. I was led to go back to Eureka Springs. They were having a big convention there with a lot of preachers, and I had received a letter from Brother Humbard just a few days before, saying he wasn't planning on going to the convention.

When Mary heard I was going back to Eureka Springs, she decided she was going with me. I told her, "Well, we don't have enough money for our tickets, but we'll put our fleece out and if we get enough money then we'll go." Wouldn't you know it, the money came right in and after we'd paid for our tickets, we only had about four or five dollars left.

When we arrived in Eureka Springs, one of the first things I heard was that Brother Humbard was there, and he had the influenza pretty bad. Uncle Jack was at the train depot as usual when I got back to Eureka Springs, and he said to me, "If you want to see Brother Humbard alive you had better hurry because he's at the point of death with influenza."

"What? I didn't even know he was here!" I exclaimed.

"He's here all right, and he's staying at the big Chautauqua Hotel."

I hurried up to the hotel and went up to see him. He looked like he was already dead when I got there. He was there all by himself; everyone had left except a couple of men. They were all trying to get away just as quick as they could. I walked into the room, and he was surprised to see me there because I was supposed to be in Carrollton.

He had had nothing to eat or drink for three or four days, and there was no one to get anything for him. I asked him what he would like to eat or drink. He thought about it for a minute or two and then said he'd like potato soup. I ran back to the school, which was only about a block away from the hotel, and got some potatoes, milk and butter. After making the potato soup, I took it back to him, and he said it was the best soup he had ever tasted.

Finally Brother Humbard got better and strong enough to

go back to his home, and I stayed at the school. There were only about sixty people left in the school, and they were all sick with the influenza except for three or four of us who were left to take care of them all.

After I had waited on people for a few days, influenza hit me, and I felt like my breast bone was breaking in two. I was really bad off, and a preacher came and prayed for me but I didn't get healed instantly.

Now there I was lying in bed, not knowing if I was going to live or die, and yet my wedding was set for the next Tuesday, Ocotober 29, 1918. Brother Humbard and I had met on Tuesday. He had asked me to marry him, and I said if I didn't get married then, I was going back to Carrollton, and forget all about it.

We had been forced to put off our wedding once. We had planned to get married at a big gospel meeting but the leaders had called us in and asked us to wait. They said, "If it's really the Lord then it won't make any difference to wait."

I said that if we didn't get married on Tuesday, October 29th, then I would go back to Carrollton and not marry any man in the world. If I didn't marry Brother Humbard, then I would never marry anyone. That's what I told Mother Barnes.

But I didn't have the money to go on, since I had spent practically all the money I had to buy juice and food to help the others. Tuesday morning came and I still didn't have the money. I was better, and was able to get up and get dressed. Here it was eight o'clock in the morning on my wedding day, and still I didn't have any money, nor was I packed, and it was quite a distance to Brother Humbard's hometown. But I really wasn't worried. I knew I would do whatever the Lord wanted. I could just stay there at the school, though I didn't have any money to eat on, but I knew the Lord would take care of me.

Suddenly there was a knock at the door, and when I answered there was a girl with a special delivery letter for me from Brother Humbard. I signed the receipt, and when I opened the letter there was money for me to travel on. I knew then that this was the Lord's will and that this was His day. So I packed, ran down to the train depot, and was on my way by eleven o'clock to Heber Springs, and that's where we were married.

Brother Humbard met me at the depot. He had the license, and had rented a room at the hotel right across from the depot. We were going to have to get up at five the next morning to catch a train to Pangburn, Arkansas, about sixteen miles from Heber Springs.

We walked through a park towards the preacher's house where we were to be married. In the middle of the park there was a little bridge that went over a small creek. When we got to the bridge, we stopped and he turned to me and said, "Now do you feel like this will hinder your ministry? I wouldn't want to do anything in the world that you feel could hinder your ministry. If you feel it will interfere with your service for God, then we can call the whole thing off."

"No, I sure don't! I feel that it's God's will. Do you feel like it will hinder your ministry? If you think that it will, I'll go back to Carrollton and forget about it," I said.

"Well, I prayed and I know it's God's will. I know you're the girl God has chosen for me," he replied.

After we talked it over we went on to the preacher's house

and he performed the ceremony. Afterwards we went back to the hotel, and got up the next morning at five o'clock to catch the train to Pangburn.

A funny thing happened that night at the hotel. It was an old plank hotel, and the door to our bedroom was kind of warped. Brother Humbard had an old skeleton key and locked it and then couldn't get it unlocked. I laughed nearly all night about him locking us in and he was up all night trying to unlock the door. He took his knife out and finally got the key out of the door, but when he tried to unlock the door with his knife he couldn't. Finally about four o'clock in the morning someone heard him trying to get the door unlocked and came to help. He had taken out the screws that held the lock in place, and when he did that the lock fell on the floor. The porter heard the noise and came running to see what happened. So they finally got the door opened and we caught the five o'clock train.

Brother Humbard had built a big church in Pangburn, Arkansas. Someone was living in the parsonage when we arrived, so we lived in a hotel until the people moved out. It was only a couple of months until their time was up and they moved out.

From the very first night of our marriage in Heber Springs in that little hotel room, we established a family altar. We knelt and prayed and asked God to help and guide us, so we could live before Him to help other people.

We were married on Tuesday and a week from that Friday they closed all the churches because of the epidemic. When I was coming down on the train from Heber Springs to Pangburn, the people on the train had all the windows open. They said they didn't want to get the influenza. I guess they thought they could freeze the germs out, but I was the one who was freezing. Tuesday was my wedding day, but on Friday I had a relapse of influenza. By Sunday morning at four o'clock, Brother Humbard thought I was dead. He said I was white as a sheet and cold as ice. I came to myself and realized the Spirit of the Lord was speaking to me. I was just lying there and the Lord said, "You have preached faith to others, now you must practice your own." But I didn't exactly understand what He meant.

During this time someone came and wanted Brother Humbard to go to a house and pray for the sick. There were nine in the family, and eight of them were already dead. People today have no idea how bad that epidemic was, but then people were dying like flies. They wanted Brother Humbard to come quickly but he said "I can't go because my wife is at the point of death. I won't leave her."

"No, go on. They need you more than I need you," I begged him, and finally he left. I went on praying and the Lord kept on impressing me that I was to go to church that night.

While my husband was gone, I got up and tried to get my hair combed and my clothes on. I was staggering around all over the room bumping into chairs and everything, trying to get dressed. I was just so weak, but finally I managed to get myself dressed.

When Brother Humbard came home he said "I wish you were well so you could go with me to pray for these people." There was such a great need and at the same time he was greatly concerned about me. With him was his brother-in-law, my husband's assistant whom I had never met before. His brother-in-law said to me, "Oh, I was hoping you would go to church tonight.''

Right then I said, "I'm going!''

I'll never forget what he said then. "If you have that much faith then I'll help you get there. I'll come and get you in my old Ford.''

"I'm going if I have to crawl!'' I insisted. I knew God had told me to go and sure enough his brother-in-law came after me that evening.

My husband had a beautiful big tabernacle which he had built two or three years before we were married. In the summertime, for camp meetings, you could push both sides out and it would be cool as spring. Closed up it would seat over a thousand people, and with the sides pushed out it would seat a thousand more outside.

That evening they helped me get into the car, and when we got to the church, they helped me up on the platform.

It was the first time I had ever been in that church, and they had to practically carry me in. Now just about every eye in that little town was on me because they had heard that Brother Humbard was getting married, and they all wanted to see his new wife. As soon as they got the news out everyone wanted to see me. In fact, they got the news out too fast. Brother Humbard had sent a picture of me to his brother-in-law to see what he thought of me. So his brother-in-law took the picture down to the newspaper office and told them Brother Humbard was married, but he didn't know who the girl was. They ran it in the newspaper several months before we even got married. Brother Humbard sent me one of the papers, and I was shocked to see myself married when I really wasn't.

Well they got me up there on the platform, and if I was going to act on faith I had to go all the way. The people were already singing. In those days they didn't just sing one or two songs and quit, but sometimes as many as a dozen with some of the choruses over fifteen or twenty times if the Lord got to blessing real good. And there I was holding myself up with one hand and my song book in the other just shaking like I had the palsy. With every eye on me, I don't know what they must have thought, but I had to obey God.

After they had sung I don't know how many songs, and my knees were popping together, someone all at once said, "Let's sing hymn number 135." Now I knew that meant "Where the Healing Waters Flow" and I was just praying in my mind. "Lord please help me, let your healing waters flow through me."

I don't know on which exact verse it happened but the power of God struck my head and went through my whole body like a streak of lightning. All at once I was strong, and never felt better in my life! I gave that hymn book a sling, and went preaching and singing all over the platform. I just walked up and down that platform praising God that I was completely healed. I've never had a touch of influenza since.

The next day I got up and started going with my husband to visit the sick people. We went right into the rooms where people were sick with the influenza, and, after praying, saw them healed. It was an experience I'll never forget.

I admit it was quite a task to go to church in front of all those people who had come to see Brother Humbard's new bride, but to get something from God, you have to go after it! He furnishes it for us, but He doesn't always bring it to us at our convenience.

Those early days of our marriage were busy ones for,

although my husband pastored the tabernacle in Pangburn, we also traveled to many evangelistic meetings. Alpha would turn the church in Pangburn over to his brother-in-law, and then we would go out.

One of our first meetings after our marriage was in Middletown, Ohio. About that time I found out I was pregnant. It was good news for both of us, and whenever I would talk about the baby that was coming, I would always tell everyone "His name will be Rex!" Rex means "king" but I didn't know that until many years later.

For twelve years we headquartered in Pangburn. We would go out every summer in evangelistic tours, and return to Pangburn in the winter. All of our children were born there except the first and the last. Rex was born in Little Rock, Arkansas.

There was a pastor friend of ours who had a mission church. Brother Humbard didn't belong to their movement, but this pastor wouldn't turn his congregation over to anyone but Alpha. This pastor, Brother Joiner, came up one day and pleaded with Brother Humbard to come and take over his church because he was leaving. Brother Humbard told him we had our own big tabernacle there in Pangburn and he asked Brother Joiner why he didn't get a preacher who was a member of his movement to take over. But no, he wouldn't settle for anyone but Brother Humbard. So we prayed about it, and determined it was God's will for us to go there after all.

We got another preacher to come up and help out at Pangburn, and we went down to help in that little mission. The people really seemed to like us and soon we had

93

outgrown the mission, and had to move out to a church on Chester Street. We stayed on Chester Street for several months and the crowds grew until finally we outgrew the church there, too. Next we found a great big church right downtown on Eleventh and Main Streets, and that's where we were when Rex was born. He was born on the thirteenth of August, nine months and sixteen days after we were married. On the thirteenth of August my husband had a big camp meeting back up at Pangburn, so when Rex was just two days old, Alpha had to leave and go to the meeting. When Rex was eleven days old, I took him to church and preached. Some of the ladies there offered to take care of the baby, but I told them "No, we're not starting him out that way." Instead I took a blanket and pillow and fixed him a bed in the preacher's chair on the platform. We sang, and I preached, and we had an altar call, and through it all he never made a sound.

So many people make a big mistake by not training their children right from the beginning. They say, "Now Johnny, if you do that again, I'm going to whip you." Then after he's done it again they say, "Now didn't I tell you if you did that again I was going to whip you? If you do it again, I am going to whip you." Well, they're just lying to Johnny and he knows it. She's already told two lies and is fixing to tell a third one. I've heard kids snicker and laugh and say, "She says that, but she won't do it."

My children were all small together, from eighteen months to two-and-a-half years apart. We continued to minister and travel around with all our children, but we didn't have any real trouble with them. They were well-behaved because they had to be. We were constantly visiting in people's homes, and we couldn't have our children running around like wild Indians.

Now I'll tell you our secret in raising children. My husband said to me, "Hon, you tell a child to do something once and ask if he heard you, and then that's all you tell him." And that's exactly what we did. I'd say, "Rex, do so and so, do you hear me?" He would say "Yes, ma'am" and do it. All of our children were like that.

From the beginning we established a family altar in our home, and prayed every day with our children. We also taught them that the Bible was the Word of God, and we didn't whitewash anything by saying, "Well now, children, both of us are ministers and work for the Lord, so you'll all go to heaven." No, we told them if they had Christ in their hearts, and lived for God they would go to heaven. If they didn't, they would be lost just like anybody else. The Bible says to train up a child. You can feed children, give them clothes and have food on the table three times a day, but that's not training them up. That's not all God means when He says "Train up a child in the way he should go, and when he is old he will not depart from it."

I started teaching Rex when he was only two and a half days old by taking him in my arms and preaching him his first sermon. Now, people will say you're crazy preaching to a little baby, but I took Rex in my left arm and used my right arm to point my finger. "Rex, you are dedicated to God and were even before you were born. You are God's child, and your life is to help others find Jesus Christ. If you live for God, Rex, it will be wonderful, and God will bless you. But remember, if you ever get away from God at any time, boy, you are in trouble.'' He just looked up at me and smiled.

Now that might sound funny but I just talked to him like he was grown and understood it. God's hand has been upon him ever since, and he's never had any other job except working for the Lord, so he must have gotten something out of that first sermon.

7

My husband always had it on his heart to build an orphanage, but he never intended to be the one to run it. Before he even started to build an orphanage in Pangburn, we had four children whom we were keeping in our home because they had been deserted by their mother and their father was in prison. At the time I already had Rex and was pregnant with Ruth, so I had quite a task on my hands trying to take care of four more. In addition we knew of other children who needed a home, so by faith my husband got busy and built the orphanage downtown.

A certain man was recommended to run the orphanage for us. He claimed he had a call on his life for that kind of work, but we ended up firing him because he was mean to the children. He had a really bad temper, so after he left we had to take over because there was no one else who could.

My husband and I knew this wasn't our real calling, but we stuck to it for some years. There were from fifty to one hundred children at the orphanage and at the same time we were still pastoring the big tabernacle. When people began to hear about the orphanage they sent us children from every direction.

When you have that many children around, something is bound to be always happening. But we didn't have a lot of trouble with the children because we loved them and saw that they were provided for. If they needed a spanking, then we would spank, but we didn't have to do that very often. We raised those children just like they were our own. And that meant no one stayed at home on Sunday morning. Everyone went to church including one little six-month-old boy.

I would get up at four or five in the morning and get everything ready for Sunday dinner. I'd bake pies or cakes, and get all the bread made and the vegetables cooked. We had a big wood-burning range, and I would put some of the things in the warming closet, and leave vegetables and the like on the back of the stove so when we came home from church they would be ready to take up and put on the table.

After I got the dinner ready, I would get everyone up and fix breakfast. Then we would all go off to church, and I would help with the service. The children would all sit there in the front rows and we never had any trouble with them. I still don't know how we did it all. It had to be with God's help.

My husband had built a big playroom in the orphanage, and after supper every evening the children would go to the playroom and play with their toys and things. Before bedtime we would get them all together, and have prayer with them and read the Bible.

We had one little boy, I guess he was about nine years old,

and every night when Brother Humbard would read the Bible, he would sit on the floor at Brother Humbard's feet and listen. He was so attentive I believe that if Brother Humbard would have read the Bible all the way through, this little boy would have sat there and listened. And every night he would say the same thing, "Brother Humbard, do you have time to read just a little bit more?" I never saw anyone who loved God's Word more. He became a great preacher I was told, and when I asked someone about him a few years ago they said he had gone to heaven. I thought, if that was the only soul that had gone to heaven as a result of those years, it would have been worth it all.

Back in those days we didn't have things very handy. I made my own soap and did the washing on the board. Yet, to tell you the truth, we had more time then than we do now. The older children would help with the younger ones, but there was still a lot of people to feed and a lot of work to do. So when I hear about people today who have only two or three children, and say how they just can't get up and take their children to Sunday school and church, it makes me disgusted.

One day I got so tired, I just felt like I couldn't go another step. I said, "Well, I've gone my limit. I can't do another thing." But that night I had a dream of heaven. In this dream, the streets were pure gold, and shone like crystal. There were flowers and perfume all over and the beauty of everything was just beyond any earthly thing I've ever seen, and I've seen a lot of this world.

I didn't see the Lord, but His presence was everywhere. You could just feel the uplifting power and presence of God. When I woke up I felt completely rested. For the next three months it was like walking on a cloud and I'd ask myself, "Am I already in heaven, or what is this?"

We had one boy by the name of Frederick, who had red hair and was kind of a mischievous little fellow. He had been adopted by a couple when he was younger, and then his foster mother died and his foster father remarried. The new wife couldn't get along with Frederick, so they brought him to the orphanage when he was about seven years old. After Frederick had grown up, he met a girl, and wanted Brother Humbard to marry them. But Alpha was gone on a trip at the time, so he asked me to perform the ceremony and I agreed. He married a precious sweet little girl just before he went into the army. They had a little boy but Frederick didn't get to see him until the little boy was two years old.

One day while we were holding meetings in Hot Springs, and had our trailer parked behind the Gospel Temple, the doorbell rang. I went to the door, but couldn't tell who it was because he had a cap on and his head was down. "Yes, can I help you?" I asked. Then he laughed, and I recognized Frederick's laugh. I pulled him into the trailer and hugged and kissed him. Then we sat down and began to talk. He told me about all the experiences he had had in the army the past years. He had a lot of close calls during the war. I finally asked if he had ever gotten saved, and he said he hadn't.

"Oh, Frederick, you've been in the army three years and went through all those things and you never got saved! Weren't you afraid you'd get killed and go to hell?"

"No, I knew that you were praying for me and I wasn't afraid," he answered.

"Well, that's not enough, Frederick. You have to give your

heart to Jesus. You can't lean on my prayers all of your life. You have to know Jesus yourself,'' I said.

I thought maybe he'd get saved that very day, but he didn't. Pretty soon he got up to leave and said, ''Well, I'll be back tomorrow.'' I wasn't sure if he'd be back or not because I had talked pretty straight with him about getting saved.

But sure enough, the next day he came back and brought his wife and their little two-year-old son. They visited for a while and then I said, ''Well, Frederick, don't you want to get saved?''

''Yes, I do!'' he answered.

I was just so happy. Here was the boy we had raised all those years just like our own, and after all that time he was finally ready to get saved! Next I said to his wife, ''Honey, don't you want to get saved, too?'' And she said yes.

Well, they knelt down in front of the divan with their little boy standing between them, and I knelt down behind the little boy and put my arms around both Frederick and his wife. I prayed, and then they both prayed and gave their hearts to the Lord right there in the trailer.

Just before we took over the orphanage, I received a letter from my friend Mary Krauss. She told me about two orphan teenage girls. They were in another orphanage, but they were very dissatisfied there. The younger girl needed a lot of attention.

Mary and her sister were in evangelistic work and couldn't keep both of the girls, so Mary wrote and asked me to take the oldest girl. She didn't want us to take the youngest because she had bad problems. Her whole body would swell up, and she'd hurt all over. Sometimes her spells would last six weeks at a time. She would have to be kept in bed with her feet propped up and be waited on hand and foot.

Well, we prayed about it, and told them we'd take the youngest girl. One day she came home from school for lunch and she wasn't feeling well. She didn't want anything to eat and she asked if she could stay home from school that afternoon. I said "Bobbie, I'll tell you what you do. You go back to school and if you don't feel better in one hour, you just ask the teacher to let you come home." As soon as she walked out the door to return to school I went into her bedroom and got down on my knees by her bed. I asked God to heal her and deliver her of this condition.

She didn't come home in an hour, but when school was out, I saw her hopping and skipping across the school yard. She didn't look like she was sick, and I believed the Lord Jesus had healed her. She came in the house with a big smile.

"Bobbie, how do you feel?" I asked right away.

"Well, when I got back to school and sat down at my desk, something went all over me and I felt really good. I knew I wouldn't have to go home because I felt so good." And she never had another sick spell after that day!

My son Clement preached his first sermon at the orphanage when he was five years old. One night all the children were gathered together in the big playroom right before the family prayer meeting. Clement came in, and he had a little New Testament in his hand. "All you children sit down," he said. Well, they all began to sit down just like he was the boss or something. Then Clement began to preach. "I want to preach a little. Now if all you children are good, you'll go to heaven. If you're bad, you'll go to hell.

Amen.'' That was his sermon. He opened his little New Testament and pointed his finger, just like he was a real preacher, and I guess he almost was.

When Rex was about two-and-a-half years old, an old preacher by the name of Brother Snyder came to our camp meeting. A couple of miles from our house was a great big bluff and Brother Snyder especially wanted to go see it. So we hitched up the old horse and buggy, some of us rode, while the others walked over to the top of the bluff. From the top, everything below looked so small.

"Rex," I said, "I'll have to hang on to you. You're so lively you might jump off." I was holding him really tight when Brother Snyder asked to hold him.

"Hold him tight, Brother Snyder," I said. "If anyone falls from here, they'll never come out alive."

Brother Snyder took Rex by the hand and began questioning him very seriously. "Rex," he said, "how come this bluff is here?" Rex backed off and with his big brown eyes looked him in the face. You could tell he was thinking.

"Rex," Brother Snyder asked again, "do you know who made this bluff?" Rex just looked up at him and said, "God said, 'Let there be a bluff' and there was a bluff!"

I've always treasured that remark because it told me how much Rex understood the things of God, even at that early age.

Rex preached his first sermon at the big tabernacle in Pangburn. During this particular service, I was sitting at the organ, and Rex was sitting up on the platform, when all at once while my husband was preaching, Rex just slipped down and got right behind him and started preaching, too. He was telling people about God, eternity, and that the Bible was God's Word.

There were steps leading up to the platform on each side, and Rex followed his daddy a few rounds and then went down the steps on the left and knelt down in the middle of the altar with his hands up over his face. Then he got up from the altar and walked up the steps on the right side of the platform and sat down. There wasn't any disturbance because it was the Spirit of the Lord. People just started weeping and crying all over the place. Some people whose hearts were hardened were actually touched by hearing this four-year-old preach.

That time in Pangburn was quite an experience for us. We had a dozen businesses going to support the tabernacle and the orphanage. We had a printing office, a gas station and a cream station. It sounds like just too much for two people to take care of, but we did it all with the help of almighty God.

While we were running the orphanage we had two more children of our own, Mary and Leona. Mary was a very sweet little baby and all the children just loved her. She was very healthy and learned to say "dada" and "mama" like most babies do when she was around four or five months old.

One day we ran out of milk, and my husband went out to the store and got another can. But the can of milk had something wrong with it, and when we gave Mary a bottle she got deathly sick. She began to throw up everything and couldn't keep anything down, not even water. While she was still getting over this, one of the little girls in the orphanage who loved Mary came in and got Mary out of her bed and started up the steps with her. My husband started after them but before he could get there the little girl dropped Mary on her back.

For over three years I had to carry little Mary on a pillow and she was nothing but skin and bones. We continually prayed for her and I was up so many times at night with her that the neighbors said it looked like we had flickering lights. I never knew from day to day if I would find her dead or alive.

I can hardly explain how I felt when I realized she was afflicted. It was an awful feeling. The worst thing was when people would gaze at her, and kids would make fun of her when she couldn't do anything for herself. That always hurt, but I kept going, I wouldn't stop my ministry at all. I never have and I never will.

A lot of people would make remarks and say, ''Well, if she prays for people to be healed, why doesn't she heal her own child?'' Well, I don't heal anybody. Jesus does that. If I could heal, I guess she would have been the first one I would have healed. I just trust God and He does the healing. I know that He has certainly been good to us, and I praise the Lord that He's given her a good mind and memory.

My husband was broken-hearted, too. He said, ''We'll just pray and not let our faith fail.'' So that's what we have done through the whole ordeal. It was really heartbreaking to see this little baby. She weighed eight pounds when she was born and weighed only nine-and-a-half pounds when she was five-and-a-half months old, so you can imagine what a little bunch of skin and bones she was.

I remember one time, after we moved to England, Arkansas, during the Depression. My husband had gone to Hot Springs to hold a revival. We were about a mile from the building where we held our services. I was preaching down there on our meeting nights and on Sundays, taking all five of the children. This was before Juanita was born.

On this day, it seemed as though I had come to the very end of my rope. Money was scarce, and we had no food. My husband had no money. He preached two weeks over there and got two dollars and a half. He couldn't send me anything and I didn't have anything.

I was sitting at the sewing machine, patching up the children's clothes. I always believed in keeping them clean even if they didn't have anything but rags. I felt like I was coming apart, completely.

I was looking out the window at the children playing. Rex had won a little red wagon from selling Bible pictures. They had Mary in the wagon; she could sit alone by that time. They would take her out with them because she enjoyed watching the rest of the children play.

I felt like I couldn't take it any longer and I said, "Lord, give me a Scripture. If it kills me, *amen*. If it helps me, *amen*!" I opened the Bible to the verse where the man was blind from birth and the disciples asked Jesus, "Who did sin, this man or his parents?" Jesus answered, "Neither this man nor his parents, but that the works of God should be made manifest."

I was down on my knees, reading this Scripture and praying. I got up and praised the Lord. I said, "Lord, the works of God can work in her, too, to the glory of God!" I felt that Scripture really saved my life! This was one of the biggest crises of my life.

The devil would still really fight me because of Mary by saying, "Well, I guess now you won't be going and praying for the sick all of the time. You've really got something on your hands."

But I answered him, "No, it's God's Word, and I'll pray for the sick until I die. God's Word is God's Word."

My husband had a cousin who was a doctor in town but he

never came to church. One day when Mary was almost six years old, he came to me and said, "I don't want to hurt your feelings, but that child will never be able to walk or do a thing. She'll be a paralyzed person all her life, if she lives at all."

Just then the Spirit of the Lord came on me and the Lord said, "She will walk." Then I said, "Dr. Pealer, Mary will walk."

"Well, if she does, I want you to bring her to see me," he said, and left.

While we were ministering in Hot Springs after leaving the orphanage, my husband announced one week that he was going to preach on unwavering faith. "God will confirm His Word with signs following my preaching" he said. He preached that whole week on unwavering faith.

There was a girl who lived not too far from us whose name was Esther. Esther was at death's door, but her people didn't come to our church at that time. They went to a church where they preached that if you were a real believer your physical body would never die. (The pastor of that church died while we were still there. I know, because I went to his funeral.) One night after services Esther's brother came and asked us to go out and pray for her.

She was real low, and they said death was near. We talked with her and read God's Word, then prayed the prayer of faith for her. Instantly God healed her. She got right up, put her clothes on and took us home in the car. There were other miracles that took place that week, but the best one of all happened to Mary. She was six years old now and had never walked. She couldn't even turn herself over or feed herself.

We had a big hall in the place we were living in that measured 104 feet long by 16 feet wide. On wash day in the winter time we put two or three clotheslines up to dry my wash on. That wash day as usual I had mountains of clothes to wash. My husband had gone to the post office and was coming back when Mary heard his footsteps at the door. Right then the Lord touched her, and she got down out of her chair and walked towards him through the hall, pushing the sheets up as she went. Alpha didn't know who it was at first, but he thought maybe Leona had come home early from school. He was just starting to ask her why she was home so early when he suddenly saw it was Mary. Now you talk about an old-fashioned shouting camp meeting. Well, we had one. We began jumping up and down and knocking those sheets and pillowcases all around.

Mary has been walking ever since. She doesn't walk as pretty as some people, but I told God if He let her walk, I'd thank Him for every step she ever took.

The Lord is wonderful, and I know He can finish what He has started. Today Mary has a great compassion for people who are sick or afflicted. She helps me pray over all the requests that come in my mail. She has prayed for many people who have been healed, some of them instantly.

Well, we finally found homes for all of our orphans except Frederick and he lived with us until he was grown. We got out of that ministry, but life wasn't dull after that. God always kept us busy and on the move for Him!

8

The Great Depression was going strong when we finally left Pangburn, Arkansas, after pastoring there for about twelve years. From Pangburn we moved to Clarendon, Arkansas, and pastored a church there for nearly a year.

We had met a businessman from Clarendon in one of our early meetings, and he prevailed on us to move down there and pastor his church. He owned the church and the land it was on, so after praying about it, we felt that the Lord would have us go there. When a year was up we started thinking about moving on. But every time we did I would look out the windows at our cow and chickens and think about what we had there.

That old milk cow gave lots of milk, and I was used to making plenty of good butter and cottage cheese. With the eggs from the chickens I knew we would always have something to eat. One Friday, I was looking out the back bedroom window at the old cow in the lot and I said to myself, "That's the best old cow we've ever had. I wouldn't mind moving if it wasn't for that old cow. But she gives so much milk and butter I'd sure hate to have to leave her!'' Now my husband would usually get up early every morning and throw some hay out for the cow, and then I would go out and milk her. On Sunday morning, he got up and went out, and the old cow was lying there stretched out on the ground, just as dead as she could be. I said, ''Well, the Lord thought, if the cow is in your way, I'll just take her away.'' And, sure enough, right after that we moved.

In 1932, we arrived in Hot Springs with five children. That made seven of us, and when Alpha counted our money, we had a total of eight cents. Here we were in a strange city without even a church yet and we had only eight cents. My husband had felt a calling to Hot Springs for a long time, and just before we moved he had made arrangements to get an old run-down theatre building that was torn up on the inside. All we could do was trust God.

Shortly after we moved in, the Lord spoke to a woman in town while she was praying and He told her to take groceries down to the New Gem Theatre which was now called the Gospel Temple. She didn't try to understand what it meant, but began to investigate and sure enough found out that we were down there trying to minister. So this lady told her sons Roscoe and Bill to go with her to the grocery store and get an order of groceries, and to take it down to the theatre.

They said ''Mamma, what's the matter with you? Why would you want to do that? The Depression is on and we don't have much money ourselves.'' But she insisted that God told her to and it had to be done. So her sons had bought the groceries and her grandson brought them in a little red wagon down to the Gospel Temple. I rejoiced in how God

110

had answered our prayers, but in one way I wasn't surprised, knowing how faithful God had always been. There was even fruit and oh, how my husband loved fresh fruit.

God continued His faithfulness in Hot Springs and we were able to rebuild that theatre building into a beautiful tabernacle for the Lord. Our youngest child, Juanita, was born there and we witnessed many other outstanding miracles.

The building alone took a lot of work. We had twenty rooms on the second floor where we lived over the church auditorium. Later we remodeled it and expanded it to twenty-seven rooms.

Now with all that room you would have thought I could have found a private place to pray, but it wasn't that easy. I would go into my bedroom, and just as I was about to pray, somebody would knock on the door, or come in to bother me. For the life of me I couldn't find a place in that big building to get alone with God. Then one day I had a thought. We had great big closets in each of the rooms and one day I found a way to fix up a place where I could really get alone to pray, a spot where nobody would be able to find me.

There were clothes hanging across the front of our closet, and boxes stored behind them on the floor. Some of the boxes were filled, but I left an empty one up front that was easy to move in and out. There was a space behind them just big enough for me to get behind, and there I could get on my knees and pray as long as I wanted to. I'll tell you, I got some prayers through then!

I would be in there just praying up a storm and I could hear people looking for me. They would knock on the bedroom door and call "Sister Humbard, where are you?" Then the

111

children would come in and try to find me. "Where's mamma? I can't find her anywhere," they'd say. Next my husband would take a spell at looking. He would even look under the bed, but I knew better than that. They never thought of looking behind the boxes, and it became a true prayer closet for me.

We had good times and bad times at the Gospel Temple, but God always sent someone along to help out. A woman by the name of Mrs. Childs came to me one day and said, "Sister Humbard, you work too hard. I want to come and help you. My son and I will come and help out for just our board." I told her we didn't have any money to pay her, but she didn't seem to care. She just wanted to do something for the Lord, so they came and lived with us for two years.

One Saturday night Mrs. Childs came up to me and said, "Sister Humbard, do you have any money? We don't have a thing for dinner tomorrow. There's not a thing in the house!"

"No, I don't have any money," I answered. If we only had fifty cents it would have bought enough to make us a good dinner, but there just wasn't anything left.

"These children have got to be fed. They are so sweet, they've just got to have food," she began to cry.

I told her to think about what food she wanted, and then to get all her cooking vessels out and put them on the stove just like she was cooking. And, if she wanted something to bake, to get those pans out too. She looked at me very strangely, and I said, "We'll just see what God will do. We'll trust Him to fill the pots for us." I was thinking of the woman in the Bible who had a little bit of oil!

Mrs. Childs did what I said and it was quite a sight to see all those empty pots and pans setting on the stove. She named off a big roasting hen with dressing, beets, and several different vegetables, and she put out pans for everything she named. I then went to the Lord and got down on my knees to pray. "Lord, we need food. We're working for you and trusting you to support us!"

Well, a strange thing happened. Early the next morning a man parked his car across the street. He came to our door and told my husband about a very strange experience he had had. Now this man had never seen us, or been in the Temple before. He lived eleven miles out in the country on a farm, and early that morning, before the sun came up, something told him to take a load of vegetables and groceries down to the New Gem Theatre. The Depression was on, but he had some money and had a lot of things stored up. He started turning and tossing in bed, and his wife asked if he was sick. "No, but as soon as the day breaks we've got to get up and go down to the garden and get vegetables."

She asked, "Are you all right?"

"Yes, I'm all right, but I've got to get up and take a load of things down to that theatre."

"Why do you want to take them down there?" she asked, thinking more and more that he was crazy. He'd never done anything like that before.

"Something told me, just as plain as could be, to take a load of vegetables and groceries down there," he insisted. So when the sun began to come up, he loaded up everything you could think of, and drove over with a whole carload of groceries. I never saw such a sight. He asked my husband if he'd like some vegetables from his farm, and Alpha quickly accepted. Mrs. Childs got to crying and shouting. He had even brought a roasting hen!

113

If we'd just take God at his Word when it says "Ask and ye shall receive, seek and ye shall find, knock and it shall be opened unto you." It's almost too simple for people. They think you have to go to college to learn about faith, but I didn't have to. God taught me. If the children's shoes were worn out, or their clothes, or there was no food on the table, whatever the need, God always answered prayer and provided.

God was faithful to meet not only our needs but also the needs of everyone who came to us. There was a man who was in trouble with the law and when he came to us, he was running from the police. He had a bullet wound in the calf of his right leg. He had run away from his wife and family and gotten into trouble. He had decided to go out to the city limits and commit suicide and as he was coming down Malvern Avenue, the street our Tabernacle was on, he heard me singing that song, "Sin Is to Blame for It All." He said to himself, "I'll just go in for a minute before I go kill myself." He came in and sat down. After I sang, my husband preached and gave an altar call and this man came down to the altar and got gloriously saved!

After the service he told us about himself. "I want to show you my leg" and he pulled up his pants leg. I tell you that was the worst looking leg I have ever seen. The bullet had gone all the way through the calf.

This poor man was so hungry for the Lord and we kept him there overnight and Alpha ministered to him. The next day they went together to the police and the man gave himself up. My husband told the police that the man wanted to turn himself in and had come to the church and gotten saved the day before. He said, "I know that this man has had a touch from the Lord and that he is not the same man today that he was yesterday.''

I don't know all the things that happened when he went to court but God did something because they pardoned the man and he went home to his wife and family. We received several letters from them and the letters always told how grateful they were and how glad he was that he heard me sing that song and that he had found Jesus. The last time we heard he had been appointed Sunday school superintendent.

"We are now the happiest family you will ever see," he wrote. "You told us to have family prayer every day and to read the Bible and that is what we are doing. Brother Humbard, I am so grateful for the work that you are doing there in Hot Springs and I know many people will come and get saved, people who need God as badly as I did."

Many of the people who came there to our church and got saved are out working for the Lord today. We had meetings almost day and night for seven and a half years; this included the revival that lasted two years and ten months without missing a single night.

As you know, Hot Springs is a National Park and thousands of people come there every year for hot mineral baths. It is a wonderful place to reach the lost for Jesus Christ. We spent a lot of time there from 1932 on. We kept it as our headquarters even when we were traveling all over the country full time. Today, if someone would write to the Humbard Family, in care of Hot Springs, Arkansas, the letter would come right here to my door, even though I have lived here in Akron for more then ten years.

Hot Springs holds a lot of memories for me and I'm not saying that we didn't have some battles but still it was worth it

115

all. God was always faithful, not only to care for and feed our family but he fed many people who came there. Many people came, uninvited, and stayed. We had thirteen beds in that building and we always tried to help people. Some of them just took advantage of us, but that didn't really matter. They would come and bring their suitcases and stay. We didn't want to hurt anybody's feelings, but I admit that sometimes it was hard going. We had to have faith for all of them.

We had one old man there. My, but he was poor. He looked half starved, he was sick and I cooked and carried food to him in his room. Even with food in short supply, we would always make sure that he got something to eat.

For years I had an awful hurting in my side and, though we had prayed, I had not been healed. There was a large lump almost as big as a football. I finally got down in bed and could not work. With me sick we could not continue to keep all those people, and so they had to move out.

I was never one to run after doctors and take medicine, but I did go and get examined by three doctors in Hot Springs and they all said I had a tumor. It was a water tumor and was getting bigger and they were afraid that it might break anytime. It didn't really scare me, I just said, "I'll trust the Lord."

When everyone else left, my husband took the poor sick old man over to the Pearlman Hotel. All he had was an old suitcase all tied up with ropes and strings. He wasn't there but a few days when he died. They opened up that old suitcase and found $8,000 in it!

There we were without any money and we had been feeding him and all those other people. We could buy six pounds of hamburger for a quarter but we couldn't get a quarter. All that time he had been pretending to be so poor and he never gave us one cent!

But God was faithful and I was healed of that tumor a short time after that. We had a lady named Minnie Bell coming every morning to take care of me. She would knock on the door and ask me if I was all right. I wouldn't tell anybody, not even my family, how I really felt. I would awake and my side was so stretched, it would be burning and itching but I couldn't scratch it or mash on it at all because of the danger of it breaking. I would just tingelate my fingers on it lightly. Every morning Minnie Bell would come in and sit down on the bed and we would talk about the Lord. She would say, "I've come to get my spiritual breakfast." After we talked a little and sang and prayed she would go around and clean up my room and get everything ready for the day.

One morning she came in and said, "What's the matter?" I told her there was nothing wrong with me because that was the truth. The Lord had healed me in the night. I had a dream that I was well. I dreamed that I went to the revival which was being held by the Medford Brothers. They were great singers and preachers. When I woke up the tumor was gone. I didn't know when it left or where it had gone but I was glad.

I have been at death's door three or four times and each time I have been instantly healed. I just trust God for my healing. One place in the Bible, Jesus talks about the children's bread. Healing is the children's bread. So, when I'm sick, I just take a big dose of the children's bread and eat my healing. I eat God's Word and He heals me. I trust Him, I have so far and He has never let me down. But I have no fight with doctors. Lots of my friends are doctors, but *my* doctor is Jesus.

From Hot Springs, we were invited to go down to Dallas,

117

Texas to help in a church. We were in Dallas only about a week when we got a letter from the bank that owned the Gospel Temple building. The letter informed us our lease was up, and the owner had an opportunity to lease the building to a theatre chain for a lot more money than we were paying. So Alpha had to go back and get all our things and store them someplace. It was a little upsetting because we had put so much hard work into that building, and had so many people coming to the services, but my husband always resorted to the faithfulness of God. He'd say, "Romans 8:28 is still in the Bible, so we'll just see what God will do."

The new tenants came in and changed everything back over to show motion pictures, but they were never able to make a profit in that building. They couldn't even make enough money to pay the light bill, and within just a few months they had to go out of business.

In the meantime we stayed in Dallas, and though I was trusting the Lord, I must admit the situation wasn't very pleasant. We had a very small third-floor apartment and of course there were eight of us. The children were going to school, and we were having services three or four evenings a week.

While we were in Dallas, a man from one of the national networks came over and offered us a weekly radio program. The radio money offer was a lot more than the one hundred and twenty-five dollars we were making, but when we found out we'd have to play all kinds of music and not stick strictly to the Lord's work, we turned it down. Besides, we would have had to advertise products over which we had no control. Next, the man approached the children, but they told him the family had always been in the Lord's work and always would

118

be. People found it hard to believe that we turned down that much money to stay together and work for the Lord, especially with our living conditions. But there was never any question in our minds.

We stayed in Texas for thirteen months, and when it was time to go, we left with only a half tank of gas and three future in-laws. For it was in Dallas that Rex met Maude Aimee, Clement met Priscilla, and Ruth met Lewis Davidson.

From Texas we returned to Little Rock and once again had no church or congregation. But actually we had everything we needed, for the Spirit of God was leading and directing our lives.

We found an empty lot on Markham Street in Little Rock and there we began to hold open-air meetings. At that time we didn't even have a tent, but God began to send people to our meetings, and we saw many saved and miracles of healing. Before long we were able to move into a big auditorium at Gaines Street and Third which could seat about fifteen hundred people.

About this time the man at the bank in Hot Springs heard we were back in Arkansas and asked us to come see him. He offered us the lease on the New Gem Theatre again because we were the only ones that had ever been able to make a go of it in the building. But we weren't interested in putting all that work back into it, only to have it taken away from us again. So the man suggested that we buy the building outright. My husband told him we'd pray about it and see if we could work out a deal.

When the man came back with his price it was five hundred dollars less than what we had decided on. Some friends loaned us the money to make the first two payments and then we paid off the rest at the rate of fifty dollars a month. We rented out rooms in the big house we had bought in Little Rock and used the rent to pay off the house and the Gospel Temple.

Again it took a lot of work to get the Temple back in condition and ready to hold meetings. This time we reworked the upstairs into twenty-seven rooms and Alpha even put up a big banner above the platform which read, "WHAT IS FAITH?" Then underneath on the next line, "TAKE GOD AT HIS WORD AND ASK NO QUESTIONS. GOD SAID IT, I BELIEVE IT, AND THAT SETTLES IT!"

When the people in Hot Springs heard we were back and fixing up the Gospel Temple, some of our old friends came along to help us out.

In the midst of building and hard work we did have a few laughs. People have often asked me what I do for recreation and I always tell them that I have a great time just serving the Lord. Nothing ever thrills me like leading a lost soul to Jesus. My husband was like that, too. He never stopped witnessing to the love and mercy of God. If he was out working on the front lawn or just around the grounds, he would talk to every person that walked by. He would ask them if they knew Jesus and just rejoice and talk to everyone.

I was always kind of lively and people had a hard time getting ahead of me. A lot of people liked to tease me and we had a couple of young girls visit us at the Gospel Temple who really enjoyed pulling jokes on people. They were always pestering me, so I kept trying to think of some way to get back at them. Finally, I remembered that someone had given my husband a wooden snake. It was carved out of wood like it was all coiled and ready to strike and it looked just like the real thing. When I found it while cleaning out the pantry one day I knew just what I was going to do while the girls were out. I slipped up and put it on their bed, right under the spread on the pillow.

That night they were acting crazy as usual, and I finally told them I was awfully tired, and wanted them to go to bed and quiet down. I went into our bedroom, and Alpha and I got ready for bed.

Pretty soon we heard the awfullest scream, and here came those girls just pounding on our door, trying to get in. They were yelling "Sister Humbard, Sister Humbard, come quick. There's a snake in our bed."

"Now there you go again with another one of your tricks. I know there's no snake in your bed. How could a snake get up here on the second floor? You're just up to one of your tricks again," I answered.

"Oh, no! No! We're not, really we're not! There really is a snake in our bed. We can even see his tongue sticking out." They were almost in tears, and they just kept calling and pleading for me to open the door. My husband said, "Hon, you'd better open the door. I think the joke has gone far enough."

So I opened the door. "All right now, show me your old snake. I'm not afraid of snakes anyway."

"Oh no, Sister Humbard, you'd better take something to kill it with. It might bite you!"

I just walked right into their room. "I'm not afraid of any old snake!" I reached over and grabbed that old snake up by the tail, and they were ready to faint. Then I showed them it was only made out of wood. "I told you no one gets ahead of me!" I laughed. They ended up having a good laugh too, but they didn't spend so much time teasing me after that.

There were many other occasions for laughter in my life. Mother Barnes's son-in-law, Brother Lawrence, would sometimes come to join in our meetings. But if anything funny happened in a meeting he'd kind of scold the people in the congregation. He was a great preacher but he lacked a sense of humor.

There was one old man who would come to our services and bring a little bitty peanut dog with him. He would sit up in a front seat, and the little dog would lie down right under the bench and stay there the whole service. One night this old man got happy. People were getting saved, and this man got to shouting. He went to shouting and jumping clear around the altar. The little peanut dog saw him and caught hold of his pant-leg. When he'd swing around, he'd swing the dog right off the floor. Brother Lawrence was sitting up there trying his best to keep from laughing. The more the man shouted the faster he swung the little dog around off the floor. He was growling and pulling back with his little front feet, while trying to hold on. Brother Lawrence got so tickled he just keeled over behind the organ.

Another humorous incident concerned an old couple who came to the Gospel Temple. The old woman wore a big straw hat with a wide crown. One night young Rex was sitting up on the platform near the back curtain. I had gone down in the audience to sit with our two little girls and when I looked up I saw Rex holding his stomach and laughing his heart out. When I caught his eye I shook my head and motioned for him to be still. But every little bit he'd turn loose again, and stoop over laughing. He wasn't laughing out loud, but I made up my mind that if he did it again, I was going to go up there and sit right by him and tell him to quit laughing or else.

Sure enough, he cut loose so I got up and sat down beside him. "You quit that laughing," I said.

"Wait, mamma, look back there at that old woman with the straw hat and her husband next to her."

So I watched this couple, and this is what happened. After a few minutes the man would fall asleep. His head would fall back and his mouth would fly open. It was an awful sight to see. Then his wife would fish a hat pin out of her hat and stick him so he'd jump. He'd not only wake up, but jump clear up out of his seat!

Well, next it would be her turn to fall asleep. Her chin would sink clear down on her breast, and she looked like she was ready to fall over. Her husband would look over and punch her with his elbow just as hard as he could. Rex would nearly die laughing. I got so tickled I couldn't hold myself. I just slipped down off the seat and laid down on my back behind that velvet curtain and laughed!

My husband found out what was going on and after the service he said to me "Now hon, it was bad enough for Rex to sit up there and chuckle, but you made it worse!"

9

When World War II broke out, we got a preacher to take over the Gospel Temple, and we started a twelve-year evangelistic tour. It took us from coast to coast and from Canada to the farthest points south. We preached to thousands of soldiers on their way to die, and thousands more who stayed behind. The harvest fields were especially ripe those years, and I'm thankful we could be used in God's purpose.

In our travels, we found that buying house trailers was less expensive and far easier than trying to find rooms for us all. Our four oldest children were married by this time, and the husbands and wives were all in the Lord's work with us. My husband always said his children didn't marry off, they married on. And we needed every one of them in the work we were doing. The children all began to sing as soon as they were big enough to stand on the platform, and today my great-grandchildren are still up there singing for the Lord.

When preachers heard we were out in the field on a

full-time basis, they began to call us to come to their cities. They knew we could be trusted to give people the Word of God, and that many people would be saved as a result of our meetings.

When we closed our meetings in a city we'd turn over to the local pastors a list of people's names who were saved. In turn, they would get with these newly saved Christians and help them find fellowship and counsel. One Friday night we had our big tent set up in Stockton, California, and I was preaching and praying for the sick. While the children were singing and playing their instruments a Filipino sailor walked by outside the tent and heard the music. It sounded pretty interesting so he came in to see what it was all about. Someone welcomed him, and he stayed for the whole service.

That night when we had an altar call, this young man came forward for prayer for his arm which had been paralyzed in an accident. I came to pray for him and said the same thing Jesus said to the man with the withered hand: "Stretch forth your hand!" He kind of shook his shoulders and stretched a little bit and then his arm went all the way up in the air. It was perfectly restored. I told him to thank Jesus and then I had to go on and pray for more people, but I meant to get back to him and ask if he was a Christian.

After the meeting was dismissed, I asked, "Where did the man go who had the dead arm?" Someone said he was right around behind the truck which we used as a platform. I walked around it and found him standing there praising the Lord and thanking Jesus for healing his arm. He was waving his healed arm in the air and shouting, "Thank you, Jesus, for making my arm well. Thank you, Jesus!"

More people ought to listen when ministers anointed of God tell them to do something. I've seen people experience great miracles this way.

In this same revival, one came forward for prayer who had a built-up shoe. His one leg was four or five inches shorter than the other. We prayed for him and the next evening, when I came in through one of the back prayer rooms, I saw a woman down on her knees crying and praying. I thought maybe she was seeking the Lord, so I knelt down beside her and said, "Sister, can I help you?"

"You've already helped us," she answered with tears rolling down her cheeks. "My husband was born with one leg shorter than the other and last night he came here for prayer. When we got home he started to get out of the car, but instead of limping on his short leg, he started walking normal. 'Something's happened!' he shouted. When we got in the house and took off his shoes, both legs were the same length!"

I tried to talk to her husband but he just kept crying and praising the Lord. They were both so overjoyed. It's wonderful to see what God can do if people will just believe and quit trying to substitute other things for the knowledge of God.

Some of the most amazing miracles I've ever seen have been those involving blind eyes that were opened. Once while we were in South Bend, Indiana, with our big tent, we had such big crowds we had to stretch the back curtain clear out to the sidewalk.

I was preaching about the two blind men who came to Jesus to get their sight restored, and all at once we heard a big commotion towards the middle of the tent. We could hear someone shouting, "I can see! I can see! I've got my sight!" A woman who had been blind for a long time had suddenly been healed. Another woman who had helped take care of her confirmed that the woman had been totally blind.

Rex finally got everyone settled down, and asked, "How many people here know this woman, and know that she has been blind for a long time?" There were a total of fifty-six people who knew her. So he asked her to come up on the platform. Rex gave her a little green-backed song book, and asked her if she could read. It had been an awful long time since she had lost her sight, but she opened the song book and began to read very fast. Before she got too far everyone started shouting, and all you could hear were people praising God.

Another outstanding miracle of healing of eyes occurred in Kansas City, Missouri. A woman came to the altar who had cataracts on both eyes. Her eyeballs looked like big white marbles. They stuck out, it was really sad to see.

We had started to pray and Rex was up at the microphone to make announcements. My husband, Clement, Leona and myself were praying for the sick. Some people came up leading this woman. She was about sixty years old and was totally blind. We gathered around her and started to pray and her eyeballs began to shake. They shook just like Jell-O and by the time we got through praying, the cataracts gave way, next to her nose, just peeled loose and hung by the side of her face.

She looked up and saw those big lights we had in the top of the tent over the platform and began to shout. She reached up to feel what was on her face and felt those old cataracts hanging there. She just gave them a sling and began

128

screaming, "I've got my sight, I've got my sight!" That really caused a lot of excitement.

We were holding meetings in Birmingham, Alabama, and having a wonderful time. As usual, on Friday nights, I was praying for the sick and afflicted. We saw wonderful, wonderful miracles take place. This special night was a cold, rainy night and the people were crowding into the tent until it was overflowing. They brought blankets and wore heavy coats determined to stay in spite of the cold.

One lady heard on the radio some of the testimonies of things that had happened in our meetings. She heard my testimony of how I was instantly healed of typhoid fever and decided that she would come and bring her little ten-month-old baby girl. The baby was born blind, deaf, and paralyzed all over. She couldn't do anything. She was just like a rag doll. She was one of the most beautiful children I had ever seen. The mother had heard all that God was doing and, as she was getting her baby ready to come to our meeting, one of her neighbors came and wanted to know what she was intending to do. The mother told her she was taking her baby to our meeting. The neighbor was horrified and tried to persuade her not to take the baby out in such weather. But the mother had faith that God could heal her baby and so, against her neighbor's advice, came anyway.

In the service that evening we were praying for the sick and the woman brought the child to the altar. She had to carry the child very carefully, bracing the child's body against her own. We prayed for the little girl and she lifted her head and looked up at the big bright lights that we had in the tent.

Clement said to the mother, "Mother, your baby is seeing!" The mother began to cry. Clement was standing behind the baby and he snapped his fingers really loud. The baby responded. She looked around at him and smiled. He said, "Mother, your baby is hearing!"

The mother was so happy, she was saying, "Is it really possible that my baby is healed?" The mother went back to her seat and as she was starting to sit down, the baby just jerked herself around and held herself upright just like any normal baby would. The mother let out a scream and said, "My baby is healed, my baby is healed!" The next morning when the mother woke up, the baby had pulled herself up in her crib and was walking around holding on to the sides like any ten-month-old child would do.

In this same series of meetings there was a little boy who was brought to our tent. He was about two years old. He had had polio and was completely paralyzed from the waist down. His one little foot was twisted almost completely upside down.

When they came in before the meeting started, Rex had shown them a seat in the front row. When I got ready to pray for him, his mother said, "Now, don't be surprised if he screams or cries when you come near him because he won't have anything to do with strangers." She also told me that the doctors had refused to operate on his little foot because it was so twisted. I asked her if she believed her son would be healed if we prayed for him and she said that she believed. You know you have to believe that God will do it and that He can do it.

I said, "Now, let's believe God for this child's healing." I prayed and stood right there and watched that little foot twist completely back into normal position. Just as straight as could be and instead of him being afraid of me, he reached his little arms up to me and I took him up in my arms and said, "Oh my, now we are going to stand," and I stood him down beside me and he could stand alone by himself.

The grandmother of the little boy lived across town and she came over every day to visit him. The day after the meeting, when she came to see him, she heard a noise before she got to the house and it was her daughter just praising the Lord. She met her mother at the door and said, "Hurry, mother, and see what the Lord Jesus has done!" When she got inside, her little grandson was running around in circles, so happy and saying, "Look, grandmother, I can walk now! I can run now." He was so happy.

The grandmother of this little boy came to the service and told me this story and that is how I know what happened.

The Lord did many miracles in Birmingham, Alabama. I imagine that some of the people who live there could tell you of some of the miracles the Lord did during our meetings.

One night the power of God fell even before we got the service started. My husband said that he saw two or three streaks of light go through the tent like lightning. This particular night there were a lot of photographers from different newspapers taking pictures. All at once a woman, who had been very crippled, jumped up and began to shout, "I'm healed, I'm not lame anymore." She was just jumping up and down. People all over the tent began getting healed. We had prayed before we even came to the meeting that night and the healings started taking place. There was quite a story in the papers about all that happened.

I guess the power must have gone throughout the whole community because Maude Aimee had decided to stay in her trailer that night and get a little rest. We had all our house trailers parked across the big four-lane highway and she said that the people in the park were lined up wondering what was going on over there because they could feel the power all the way over there.

The power was so strong, you could feel the mighty rushing of the Holy Spirit, like a mighty wind throughout the tent. Now, Jesus does that, not the Humbard family. Jesus uses our faith to believe God for miracles. That's the way it is.

One February evening during a revival in Augusta, Georgia, Juanita, Mary and I were hurrying to the service which was due to start in a few minutes. As we neared the auditorium, a black lady came hobbling along the sidewalk all humped over and hardly able to walk. I thought to myself how thankful I ought to be for good health, and the fact I could walk through the snow.

We passed each other in back of the auditorium and I touched her on the shoulder and said, "Don't you know that Jesus Christ can make you well?"

She stopped and looked over at me. "I never heard anything like that," she said.

"Well you believe there's a God, don't you?"

"Oh, yes, I believe there's a God!"

"Then don't you know he has the power to heal people and make them well?"

She looked so miserable standing there in the cold snow. I continued, "The Lord can make you well if you will believe Him, but you have to believe Him and have faith. The Lord told us to lay hands on the sick and they shall recover. But I don't ever pray for anybody unless they want me to."

She looked up at me and said, "Yes, I'd like you to say a

132

prayer for me!'' So I just laid my hand on her shoulder, right there in the middle of the sidewalk with the snow and wind blowing all around us. As I prayed she straightened up and shouted, ''Why didn't somebody tell me this before?''

She went down the street and we had to hurry on to the meeting. She kept looking back and hollering and waving at me. ''I never knew it before. I never knew it before! Oh, I feel so good.'' She was walking and skipping like a sixteen-year-old girl.

During the war as we traveled from city to city, we experienced a great deal of persecution. Almost every day we would hear over the radio and from different sources, how we were just raking in the money. Our opposition told people we were getting rich. To set the record straight, with all our families living in house trailers, it took everything we had to get to the next city. It took a lot of money, but it was worth it to see thousands of souls come to the Lord.

Once we were in Pensacola, Florida, and we didn't have enough money to get to the next place where we were supposed to go. We had to stay there two or three weeks extra because we didn't have money to go on. We were really getting down to the bottom of the barrel. Even our food was getting short. One day a preacher came to us and told my husband, ''The war is on and we have money laid up in the bank to build a new church, but Brother Humbard, the Lord told me that you had a great need. I'll loan you three thousand dollars.''

With that money we went to Birmingham, Alabama. The Lord helped us and enough money came in during that meeting to pay back the loan. If people think that the

Humbard family is ever out just for the money, they have another thought coming. No Humbard has ever been rich and I don't guess ever will be. If we do get money, we give it away to someone in need or put it back into the Lord's work. At that time we had a lot of big equipment, five house trailers and about twenty-five mouths to feed. If you don't think that didn't take some money. . . . But it was worth it because we saw thousands of souls come to the Lord.

We have had a lot of persecution but we have met a lot of wonderful people and had a lot of good offers. One time we were out in California, when a man and his wife came to see us and asked us if we would like to take a ride and see some sights. They wanted us to see their city and, even though we were pretty busy, my husband said he would like that.

They drove around awhile, just showing us all the sights, through Hollywood. It was really beautiful. We went through a section where there were many big beautiful homes. We came to a house, the most beautiful house I had ever seen.

There were roses climbing up the tall wall on either side of the walk and a beautiful green sloping lawn and at the top of the hill was a big mansion. Oh my, it was pretty. We were talking about how beautiful it was and the man said, "How would you like to live here?" I kind of laughed and said, "I don't think that I would know how to act in a place like that."

The man turned to my husband, "Reverend Humbard, I'll tell you what my wife and I have decided. If you and your wife and family want to live here, you can just move in and we'll give you a deed to that house. You can stay here so that we can have a good time, fellowshiping together and as long as you live, you won't have to pay one cent. The only thing that we want is just that you move in there and live the rest of your life so that we can all be together.

"Well," my husband said, "we couldn't do that. God has called us to preach the gospel and we have to keep on going." So we always went what you might call the rough road. We turned down that offer and all the other offers we had. We knew what God called us to do and we did it.

You know, friends, the things of this world, and time, soon pass away. Don't pin your faith or expectations on *just* things because it doesn't pay. Life is for living but death is for sure. I feel Jesus is coming back sooner than we think. Let's make up our minds that we're all going to heaven and there we can rejoice in the presence of Jesus for ever and ever.

As evangelists, we were used to traveling around a lot and staying in different homes. And we found we weren't always as welcome as we hoped to be. My husband's favorite Scripture was Romans 8:28, and when the situation would get a little uncomfortable, he'd say, "Remember, hon, Romans 8:28 is still in the Bible." At one time in particular, we stood on that Scripture, and God showed us the truth of the Word as well as the confirmation of His leading in the teaching of our children.

We were invited to one church to preach, and they had made provisions for us to stay with one of the families. It seemed to be the pattern that whenever a visiting preacher would come, they would be housed with different members of the congregation. The family we were to stay with was not happy with the prospect of putting up with two preachers and five children. When we got to their farm on the appointed day, we discovered there was no one home.

So we parked beside the house, and spread a quilt out on the ground. My husband and I lay down on the quilt with little

Mary between us, and let the other children play by the car. They played quietly around the car and after a couple of hours, around five in the afternoon, the woman came back to her house from the fields. She didn't even greet us, or invite us to come in. We could hear her in there fussing around and talking to herself, but loud enough for us to hear. "Well, we got that preacher and them five kids here to tear up the place," she was raving.

I told my husband, "Let's get in the truck and get away from here. I don't want to stay here!"

"Now just sit still," he said. "Remember Romans 8:28." I couldn't see it at the time, but I decided to wait and see what would happen.

The woman didn't come out and offer us a drink of water or anything; she just continued raving to herself inside. They had a beautiful garden with all kinds of beautiful vegetables, but when her husband finally called us in for supper, the only thing she served us was cold corn bread and water gravy.

It was getting late and there were five children to get cleaned up for church and we had to drive five or ten miles to the church. Finally, I went to her and said, "Sister, if you don't mind, I'll just spread a quilt here by the door and the children can lie down."

I knew they wouldn't bother anything, but before I could even finish the sentence she said, "No, you can't leave those kids here to tear up everything in the place!"

Now we had been tired and thirsty when we got there, but I wouldn't even let the children look for a drink of water until she had gotten home. She had plenty of cows with lots of good milk, but she didn't even offer my children any. Anyway, we got the kids cleaned up and went to church that

136

night.

We had taught the children a little song, "Keep Sweet, Keep Sweet," and they sang that song. It was really appropriate, but I had a heavy heart about this time.

The next morning, when we heard someone up, Ruth and I got up and went down to help. The woman fixed a little breakfast and I set the table and helped as much as I could. After breakfast Ruth and I did the dishes and made the beds. There were some buckets and water jars sitting on the back porch, so we had Rex and Clem draw water from the well and fill all the buckets and jars for her.

When she got back from milking the cows and saw all we had done, she seemed a little surprised. "Well, I'd better shell some peas. It'll probably take an hour or so to shell enough for this gang." I called the children all in and told them we were all going to help her. That was something new to them, and in about ten or fifteen minutes we had them all shelled. The kids had a lot of fun, and this time she fixed us a good dinner with vegetables and meat.

After dinner Ruth and I washed the dishes. My husband said he was spreading our quilt out on the side so we could pray for the meeting tonight. Before I went out I told the kids they could play around our car but not to get loud.

Alpha and I went out and were lying on the quilt with Mary between us, praying for the service when all at once we heard the front screen door slam. Then we saw this woman running around the house bawling. She fell down on her knees, and threw her arms around me. Here she wanted us to forgive her for everything she had said and done. She said we had the best children she ever saw in her life and that they hadn't touched a thing in her house.

I told her we stayed in a lot of homes, and the children never touched anything unless we told them to, and yet they still had a good time. They could stay in her house for a month, and they'd never open a drawer or touch a thing without being told. Romans 8:28 is right. "All things work together for good to them that love God, to them who are the called according to his purpose."

"The Love of God in Christ" was one of my favorite songs to sing during our services. One young man who came almost every night made the comment that he wished he could be as happy as I was when I sang that song. He'd come to the altar and pray but he wouldn't get saved. I don't know how many times he came to the altar without getting saved. He came to the altar one night and wouldn't leave. My husband stayed on with him there until the fire in the stove was getting low and yet the young man wouldn't leave. He said he couldn't go home until he got saved and it seemed like he couldn't get through to his satisfaction.

Finally my husband stood up and said, "I'll go back and stir up the fire in the living room, and we can go in there and pray." I had already gone back and put Rex and Ruth to bed, and was just lying down to sleep when my husband came in and said, "Hon, slip into your clothes and come into the living room. That young man won't go home until he's saved."

I got dressed and went in to pray with him. It was well past midnight when he finally said, "I'll tell you what it is. There's just one thing that's keeping me from being saved. One day I was walking up the street when I spotted a big pile of apples in Mr. Armstrong's grocery store down on Main

138

Street. They were right in the front window and I thought 'I'd sure like to have one of those big red apples.' So I found something to pry the window open and three or four of the apples fell out. I pushed the window down and went on my way with the apples in my pocket. Now every time I go to pray those apples are right in front of me. I just can't get saved until I get it straightened out."

Alpha told him, "Now, if you're earnest about this, God will save you on credit until you can see Mr. Armstrong and make it right. You tell the Lord that you'll pay Fred Armstrong for those apples, and God will save you."

Well, the boy did just that and soon felt the full assurance that God had saved him. The wonderful part was that God was calling him to preach the gospel. He's been preaching the gospel for years. He goes all across the country preaching. He has three or four churches where he preaches on a regular basis.

I never get over being amazed at what God can do! God's ways never get old to me. That's one of the reasons I continue to say, "I'm so glad that I'm a servant of the living God! My God is able to do all things."

It was in Northern California that we had an experience I still don't fully understand. We had a big revival lined up in Portland, Oregon, and the rest of the family had gone on ahead to set things up. We had remained behind to make sure all the bills and things had been cleared up. My husband never left a city owing anybody anything. A cold rain was falling as we started out with our house trailer. Fortunately Mary and Juanita were riding with us in the car, for suddenly a big truck ran into the back of our trailer. It hit so hard it reared up on end. If God had not sent His angels to look over us it would have come down right on top of our car. Somehow it went off to the side and flipped completely over. None of us were injured except for my husband.

There we were in the middle of nowhere, and we couldn't tell how badly he was hurt. All we could do was get a quilt out of the trailer and cover him up. Our trailer was demolished and everything we owned was ruined. Help finally arrived and Alpha was taken to the hospital in Redding, California. We were about twenty-five miles from Redding, with another six hundred miles to go to our next meeting. He stayed in the Redding Hospital for three days before they sent him on a stretcher by train to another hospital in Portland, Oregon. There he lay with a broken hip for six months.

When I think back to that night of the wreck, it was worse than a nightmare. God had His hand on us, otherwise we would have all been killed. My husband walked with a limp for the rest of his life, but it didn't really slow him down. At the end of six months he was back on the road with us, fervently reaching souls for Jesus. We preached in army camps and prisons to all classes of people, from the very rich, to the very poor. We've prayed for movie stars and down-and-outers. Every place it was the same thing, and sin is to blame for it all. Things haven't changed. There's still sin, but even more, there are still a lot of people hungry for God and wherever there are people hungry for God that's where I'll go and preach.

We continued to travel around the country for several years after the war, and finally ended up in Akron, Ohio, with our big family, four house trailers, trucks and the big tent.

It usually took a week to get that big old tent set up and ready for six thousand people, but if we had to move fast, we

140

could take it down and have it ready for services in twenty-two hours. At first we set up for a while on the Soap Box Derby grounds. We were there for five weeks and scores of people were saved, in spite of the opposition.

It was amazing the lengths some people would go to. We'd get some real ugly phone calls. But we knew that God had called us to work for Him and nothing could ever stop that.

Rex got the feeling that the Lord wanted him to stay in Akron and, looking back over the past twenty-five years, it seems he made the right decision. After Rex decided to stay, Clement took the big tent and continued to travel and preach for awhile before he felt the Lord's call to build a tabernacle in Youngstown, Ohio.

10

The children and their families began to establish the individual work God was leading them into. For the first time the family went separate ways, though not really, because they were all going God's way. Ruth and her husband, Lewis Davidson, had been taking care of the Gospel Temple in Hot Springs, but now they, too, were feeling God's leading to come north to Ohio.

Dad, Mary, and I went back to Hot Springs to once again preach in our old home, the Gospel Temple. Juanita had married and remained in Ohio, so just the three of us moved back into that big building. It was nice to be back among our old friends, and see God moving miraculously as usual. Hot Springs, Arkansas is an international attraction and people from all over the world come to bathe in the healing waters of the natural mineral springs that flow out of the mountains. It's a great place to reach people with the saving news of Jesus Christ.

At a camp meeting in Georgia, we had one old woman who

had peculiar ideas about chasing the devil. She was a real good pianist, and played for a lot of the camp meetings. One day when she came to the young people's meeting to play the piano for us, she laid her Bible and two revolvers down on the altar bench. She had two guns fastened to her Bible with rubber bands.

Seeing this, I walked over to the piano and said "Sister, why do you have those guns on the Bible?"

"Why that's to scare the devil!" she exclaimed.

I thought that was awful, but then she explained they were only toy pistols.

They sure looked real to me. "You can't run off the devil with toy guns," I told her, and finally had to preach a sermon to convince her. You'll never run the devil off with toy guns, it takes the real power of God. And even then the Lord said to resist the devil, not fight him. The trouble with a lot of people when temptation comes along and knocks at their door, they just say, "Come right in, Mr. Devil, and have a seat." But to my mind resisting the devil means turning and getting away from his tricks.

While we were ministering back in Hot Springs a young missionary came to visit with us. I was up preparing breakfast one morning and Alpha came in and sat down at the table. He said he only wanted grapefruit for breakfast, and then began talking to our young missionary friend about fixing one of our cabinets. It looked as though it was pulling away from the wall, and he thought that putting in another screw would make it more secure.

They finished their breakfast, and Alpha began to take the things out of the cabinet to make it easier to work with. I was at the stove in the kitchen and when I turned to watch them

Alpha was mumbling and stumbling backwards. We grabbed hold of him and helped him into the living room to a big easy chair. He said he couldn't see, but after a few minutes his eyesight seemed to clear up, and he asked for the newspaper. I brought him the paper, and he started to read it when, suddenly, he fell out of the chair.

I called our visitor and we got him into bed. He was still conscious, but when they wanted to take him to the hospital he refused. He just looked up at the ceiling and smiled. "Wonderful, wonderful, wonderful," he kept repeating. It was as though he was seeing something we couldn't see. He would wave his hands in the air and say "I love you, Jesus. I preached the Word all of my life, just the way He wanted me to preach. I didn't change a thing. Just the way He wanted me to."

I stayed beside him for several days, and he never had any pain. He just kept praising God as long as he had a voice. After a few days he lapsed into a coma, and we took him to the hospital. He was in a coma for about nine days and then, as Clement stood at the side of the bed reading from Thessalonians and I sat holding his hand, the angels came and took him home. He was just lying there with his eyes open and his lips slightly parted as though seeing something wonderful. Then his eyes and lips closed, and I knew that when we met again, it would be at the throne of God!

It was a beautiful experience. The vacuum he left behind in our lives, and in the lives of thousands of his friends, would never be filled, but we knew we'd all be together again!

My husband is one man that lived what he preached every day of his life. He was closer to God than any man I've seen. He would fast almost every week for two days. And he fasted longer at one stretch than any man I have ever heard of, eighty-seven days. I know some people say it is impossible, but I was with him continually. He lost fifty-six pounds in the process.

During the time of dad's long fast we were in a meeting at the oldest campground in the country. It is inter-denominational and they hold it every year around August 15th. Things really happened at that meeting. They had never had a time of really praying for the sick. One night while Alpha was preaching, he stopped and pointed his finger at me and said, "Hon, come now, we're going to pray for the sick." There were real miracles happening there.

The meeting went on for about ten days. The whole camp-ground was trembling under the power of God. People were asking and wondering what was going on, what was causing this mighty move of God's power. Brother Oliver Russell, the president of the campground, stood up at the evening meeting and said, "People are asking about what is happening on this campground. There is a strange holy feeling."

He pointed over toward our cabin—I never will forget it—and, with tears flowing down his cheeks, said, "I'm going to tell you what's happening. An old saint of God called A.E. Humbard is here preaching. That is why you feel the power of God in this place."

This is the kind of testimony that my husband left behind.

With Alpha gone home, I took over the full ministry of the Gospel Temple and responsibility for our rental property over in Little Rock. I think my husband knew the Lord was about to take him home, for he had begun to show me how to handle the business end of everything about two years before. At that time I didn't know how to drive a car, so I made all the hospital calls and visitations either by public transportation or on foot. For the first couple of years I did all right, but then I began to get physically tired.

One night I went to bed and I was so tired I thought I couldn't go on. I just wished the Lord would take me home so I could get some rest. The next morning, just as the sun came up, I woke up and heard someone singing the most beautiful song. I was wondering who in the world was singing at this hour of the morning when all at once I realized it was me. I was singing a song that the Lord had given me and the words were:

There's a new day that's just about to dawn, there's a new day that's just about to dawn.

This old world has sin and sorrow but there'll be a bright tomorrow.

There's a new day that's just about to dawn, there's a new day that's just about to dawn.

When it comes we'll all be traveling on.

We'll be on our way to glory, to fulfill that sweet old story of the new day that's just about to dawn.

I got up feeling so rested, and looking forward to the day and work the Lord had called me to. Once again I was saying, "I'm so glad I'm a servant of the living God."

After ministering on foot for about three years, a friend came up and offered to teach me to drive. Here I was past sixty and just beginning to drive a car. The Lord must have given my friend real courage! Talk about the ministry of helps, she was a big help.

I get a blessing out of watching helps work in the church,

and one day I had a special experience with this ministry. I was all dressed up in my best clothes and had been out taking care of some business.

By the time I walked back to the church the wind was blowing like a small gale across the parking lot. Someone had thrown a little rug there by the back door for people to wipe their feet on before they came into the building. It was a good idea because we had just carpeted the aisle in the church, and this helped to protect it. But that little throw rug had gotten pretty dirty, and I thought to myself, "Now why on earth doesn't one of those men take that rug and shake it out." Here I was arguing with myself about why some of the men in the church didn't shake out the rug.

As I stood there looking at that old rug a little voice inside me said, "Why don't you shake it out?" It just seemed like someone was standing there talking to me. So I picked up the rug and began to shake it. The wind was blowing the dirt away from me, and I kept shaking it and thinking about all the people who walked over that rug, and then came into the church and went down to the altar to get saved. Those people wiped their feet on that rug and now I was shaking the dust off. The Bible says, "Whatsoever you do in word or deed, do all in the name of Jesus." So I said, "I'm shaking this rug for Jesus!" And the more I shook it the happier I got. Pretty soon I was just running over with joy, and got to shouting, "Glory be to God! Hallelujah!"

After a while, I saw some people gathering on the street. But I was too busy shaking that rug and having a good time with the Lord to think what people might say. Pretty soon I heard someone say, "Oh, that's just Sister Humbard getting happy." I had two crowds of people standing there watching me shake that rug and believe it or not, I got a lesson out of it. We may not all do big things, but all of us can do little things. We can dust the church benches, and praise God that somebody is going to sit down on them, hear the gospel and maybe get saved. We ought to be watching all the time to see what things we can do for the Lord.

A woman came to Hot Springs to bathe in the mineral springs, and heard that people got healed at the Gospel Temple. She called and talked to me but I had a real hard time understanding her heavy accent. After a little conversation, I made arrangements to pick her up at the hotel and bring her back to the Temple. I had a woman visiting me from Akron, Ohio, and she drove me over to get this woman. As we talked on the way back to the church, I discovered that this woman was Jewish. She had come to this country from Israel. I talked to her about Jesus being able to heal her, but she said she didn't believe in Jesus. She didn't tell me what her illness was, but she had a terrible-looking growth on the side of her face. She insisted she couldn't accept Jesus so I told her that I couldn't pray for her because it was Jesus who healed, not me. Then I went through the Old Testament with her and showed her the promise of His coming, and many Scriptures about His work in the Old Testament. Finally she was able to say, "Now I see!" and wanted to pray and accept Jesus as her Messiah. Then I prayed for her to be healed in the name of Jesus.

When we drove her back after the service and stopped in front of her hotel, she put her hand up to her face and she said "My face has feeling in it. It tingles!" She touched her cheek and found the growth was completely gone. Her skin was beautiful and healthy, where just a short time before had been this terrible-looking sore which she then told us was cancer. I didn't know where it went. I looked in the car, thinking maybe it had just dropped off, but I could never find a trace of it.

In 1962, Rex called me from Akron. All he would say was, "Mamma, I want you to pray." So I called Mary in and said, "Let's pray. Rex has a burden, and I think he needs some financial help." We got down on our knees and, after praying through, Mary went into her bedroom and prayed for two more hours, just groaning and crying out to the Lord. I knew that God had heard her prayers, and in just a few days I got a call from the school board in Little Rock. They wanted to buy our old home there and I was able to sell that property and get enough money to help Rex save the Cathedral. It's like the old song says, "What a friend we have in Jesus, all our sins and griefs to bear. What a privilege to carry [not just one thing] but *everything* to God in prayer."

I stayed there in Hot Springs and pastored the church for eight years after Brother Humbard's homegoing, but my children were all in Ohio urging me to come north. So once again I turned the Gospel Temple over to another minister and left to join them. Brother Humbard had once prayed that nothing would prosper in that building except the Lord's work, and that's what happened until finally the building was torn down.

We saw a lot of wonderful things happen there, and a lot of people who heard the words of salvation for the first time in that place have gone out into the world telling the Good News.

11

When most people reach my age, and have seen their children grow up, they're ready to settle back into an easy chair. There's always a temptation to take it easy and be satisfied with past accomplishments, but I'd rather be "refired" than retired.

The little house which Mary and I call home is within a sight of Rex's giant Cathedral of Tomorrow, and every Sunday I know that millions are being reached for Christ through the services which are telecast and aired throughout the world. Each week they reach more than Alpha and I ministered to in an entire lifetime, but yet, I still can't be content to stay home and rest on my laurels.

So a good part of the year you'll find me on the road—preaching the old-time gospel in all its power and glory. Though I no longer travel with the family, or preach in a tent, and the churches are often smaller than our old Gospel Temple, the thrill and joy of serving my Lord is stronger than ever. With Mary backing me up with prayer at home, I'm seeing both young and old come to Christ just like in the "good old days."

People think I should stay home in a rocking chair, but Christ has been my whole life, and I can't stop now with heaven just in sight. The thought of someday soon going on to be with the Lord and my departed loved ones is enough to keep me going between services.

In fact, some of my most precious moments come while traveling from one church to the next when I can close my eyes and relive some of the happy memories God has given me.

Like Paul, I can say I've run the race, and am now looking forward to the things of heaven.

My mind drifts back to a favorite incident that underlines my whole life and hope for the future.

In 1960, I was pastoring the Gospel Temple in Hot Springs, only a few months after Dad Humbard had gone home to be with the Lord. I was very lonely and my mind was on heaven and the Lord most of the time. Every Saturday I would ride the bus sixty miles over to Little Rock to collect the rent on our house there.

As it happened this day, I was one of the first people on the bus. I walked back and sat down and a lady who got on right after I did came back and asked if she could sit next to me. This sort of surprised me because there were a lot of empty seats on the bus for her to choose from, but she wanted to sit next to me. Well, I didn't mind so I just scooted over to make room for her.

My mind was still on the Lord, and I just continued to gaze out of the window, thinking about what it would be like when I, too, went home.

Once the bus started moving, the woman next to me began to talk. Of course, she asked the most natural question in the world.

"Do you live here in Hot Springs?"

"Yes, ma'am. I live right down the street from the bus station but it won't be long until I'll be moving to another city."

"Are you going to move to Little Rock?" she asked.

"No, ma'am, I'm not moving to Little Rock. I'm moving to a far better place than that. A friend of mine, the best friend I ever had, has given me a mansion!"

"You mean, he just gave you a mansion?"

"Yes, he gave it to me absolutely free. I didn't pay a cent."

I could see I had really gotten her interested and her excitement was building. "Oh," she said, "I've never heard of anything so wonderful! Are you going to move into this mansion?"

I like to see people get excited, but I figured she'd catch on in a minute. I was just going to give her another hint or two, and surely she would know what I was talking about.

Her next question was, "Well, then, it's not in Little Rock?"

"No, ma'am, it's not in Little Rock. It's in the most beautiful city you've ever heard of."

"Well, I'd love to see your mansion." (I could tell that inside she was jumping up and down.)

Then I began to tell her about the city, watching her expression for the moment when she would realize where this place was. "Lady," I said, "in that city the streets are paved with pure gold, and the walls are covered with precious jewels."

153

She still didn't understand. I kept on describing the city, telling her about the twelve gates of the city, and how each gate was a great pearl. The other people on the bus were getting interested in our conversation, and some of them moved closer so they could hear better. There was a real feel of expectation on the bus.

She had listened to the description but still didn't seem to know what I was talking about. "Well, listen," she said, "when you get moved into this mansion, would you allow me to come and see you?"

I couldn't believe that anyone would still not understand what I was talking about.

"Yes, you can come, but first there are some requirements. You have to get ready to enter a place like that." I felt like every person on the bus was holding his breath. "If you're not already a Christian, you have to become one. You'll have to accept Jesus into your heart as your Savior, and when you do, He'll prepare you to come to that city, called heaven, to be with Him."

It was really amazing to me. She acted as if she'd never heard of Jesus or heaven. I could hardly believe anyone in this country could be so ignorant about the Lord.

Before I could explain any further, the bus pulled up at my stop. Almost regretfully, I stood and walked to the open door, and so caught up was I with the thought of heaven, that it was like stepping through the pearly gates themselves. Behind me, my fellow travelers still clung to the edge of their seats. There seemed to be a touch of heaven on my friend's face as she sat there, considering God's great promise.

When I get to thinking about heaven, I tell you I get so happy I can hardly wait. Oh, what a day that will be! You talk about family reunions, I've been to some wonderful get-togethers of kinfolk in Missouri and Arkansas, but that's nothing to compare with that great day that's coming!

There have been those times of heartache when I thought I couldn't go on without my beloved husband at my side. I've missed him so. But those tears turn to joy every time I catch a glimpse of heaven.

It won't be long. We'll be together again, and this time, for eternity!

There's someone else I'm looking forward to seeing there, and I have shared this with very few people.

I lost a baby between Mary and Juanita. In my eighth month of pregnancy, I no longer felt any movement from the baby and I knew there was something seriously wrong. When he was born, the doctor said he had been dead for about six weeks. I was so disappointed at losing the baby after carrying him all those months, and then never even getting to hold him in my arms.

About a year ago, I had a wonderful thing happen to me that healed all the anguish of that experience. I had just settled down at home for the evening, and was lying in bed, reading the Scriptures. Something made me turn my head to the side, and there in a half-kneeling position was a young boy.

He appeared to be about fifteen or sixteen years old and had beautiful brown eyes just like all my children have. He was so beautiful and a love rose up in my heart, a mother's love. I just wanted to reach over and take him in my arms, and I thought to myself, ''Who are you?''

The Spirit of the Lord answered my question, ''He is your son. He has gone to be with Jesus, but I want you to know he will meet you there. He's waiting for you now."

So I know now that when I get to heaven, I'll see my son and recognize him because he came to me that evening.

I'll greet my precious mother, too, whose prayers have followed me all the days of my life. And then we'll look for the rest of the family, one by one, as they come home. We'll be singing around the throne, not only the Humbard family, but the heavenly host and the whole family of God. Among them will be counted the multitude of blood-washed saints who found their way to heaven through the ministry God has blessed us with these many years.

When we stand there in the presence of our Lord and hear the angelic choir singing that triumphal anthem, we'll know it was worth every mile, every step, every heartache.

In that moment, my mother's promise from Revelation will ring loud and clear:

"Martha, be thou faithful unto death and Christ shall give thee a crown of life."